OTHER VOLUMES IN THIS SERIES

John Ashbery, editor, *The Best American Poetry 1988*

Donald Hall, editor, *The Best American Poetry 1989*

Jorie Graham, editor, *The Best American Poetry 1990*

Mark Strand, editor, *The Best American Poetry 1991*

Charles Simic, editor, *The Best American Poetry 1992*

Louise Glück, editor, *The Best American Poetry 1993*

A. R. Ammons, editor, *The Best American Poetry 1994*

Richard Howard, editor, *The Best American Poetry 1995*

Adrienne Rich, editor, *The Best American Poetry 1996*

James Tate, editor, *The Best American Poetry 1997*

Harold Bloom, editor, *The Best of the Best American Poetry 1988–1997*

John Hollander, editor, *The Best American Poetry 1998*

Robert Bly, editor, *The Best American Poetry 1999*

Rita Dove, editor, *The Best American Poetry 2000*

Robert Hass, editor, *The Best American Poetry 2001*

Robert Creeley, editor, *The Best American Poetry 2002*

Yusef Komunyakaa, editor, *The Best American Poetry 2003*

Lyn Hejinian, editor, *The Best American Poetry 2004*

Paul Muldoon, editor, *The Best American Poetry 2005*

THE
BEST
AMERICAN
POETRY
2006

◇　◇　◇

Billy Collins, Editor

David Lehman, Series Editor

SCRIBNER POETRY

NEW YORK   LONDON   TORONTO   SYDNEY

SCRIBNER POETRY
1230 Avenue of the Americas
New York, NY 10020

SCRIBNER POETRY and design are trademarks
of Macmillan Library Reference USA, Inc., used under license
by Simon & Schuster, the publisher of this work.

For information about special discounts for bulk purchases,
please contact Simon & Schuster Special Sales: 1-800-456-6798
or business@simonandschuster.com

Manufactured in the United States of America

1   3   5   7   9   10   8   6   4   2

ISBN-13: 978-0-7432-2967-8
ISBN-10: 0-7432-2967-3
ISBN-13: 978-0-7432-5759-6 (Pbk)
ISBN-10: 0-7432-5759-6 (Pbk)

CONTENTS

Foreword by David Lehman ix

Introduction by Billy Collins xv

Kim Addonizio, "Verities" 1

Dick Allen, "'See the Pyramids Along the Nile'" 2

Craig Arnold, from "Couple from Hell" 3

John Ashbery, "A Worldly Country" 5

Jesse Ball, "Speech in a Chamber" 7

Krista Benjamin, "Letter from My Ancestors" 8

Ilya Bernstein, "You Must Have Been a Beautiful Baby" 10

Gaylord Brewer, "Apologia to the Blue Tit" 12

Tom Christopher, "Rhetorical Figures" 14

Laura Cronk, "Sestina for the Newly Married" 16

Carl Dennis, "Our Generation" 18

Stephen Dobyns, "Toward Some Bright Moment" 20

Denise Duhamel, "'Please Don't Sit Like a Frog, Sit Like a Queen'" 22

Stephen Dunn, "The Land of Is" 24

Beth Ann Fennelly, "Souvenir" 26

Megan Gannon, "List of First Lines" 28

Amy Gerstler, "For My Niece Sidney, Age Six" 30

Sarah Gorham, "Bust of a Young Boy in the Snow" 34

George Green, "The Death of Winckelmann" 36

Debora Greger, "My First Mermaid" 40

Eamon Grennan, "The Curve" 42

Daniel Gutstein, "Monsieur Pierre est mort" 44

R. S. Gwynn, from "Sects from A to Z" 46

Rachel Hadas, "Bird, Weasel, Fountain" 49

Mark Halliday, "Refusal to Notice Beautiful Women" 51

Jim Harrison, "On the Way to the Doctor's" 53

Robert Hass, "The Problem of Describing Color" 55

Christian Hawkey, "Hour" 56

Terrance Hayes, "Talk" 58

Bob Hicok, "My career as a director" 60

Katia Kapovich, "The Ferry" 63

Laura Kasischke, "At Gettysburg" 65

Joy Katz, "Just a second ago" 68

David Kirby, "Seventeen Ways from Tuesday" 70

Jennifer L. Knox, "The Laws of Probability in Levittown" 73

Ron Koertge, "Found" 75

John Koethe, "Sally's Hair" 76

Mark Kraushaar, "Tonight" 78

Julie Larios, "Double Abecedarian: Please Give Me" 80

Dorianne Laux, "Demographic" 82

Reb Livingston, "That's Not Butter" 84

Thomas Lux, "Eyes Scooped Out and Replaced by Hot Coals" 86

Paul Muldoon, "Blenheim" 87

Marilyn Nelson, "Albert Hinckley" 88

Richard Newman, "Briefcase of Sorrow" 89

Mary Oliver, "The Poet with His Face in His Hands" 90

Danielle Pafunda, "Small Town Rocker" 91

Mark Pawlak, "The Sharper the Berry" 92

Bao Phi, "Race" 94

Donald Platt, "Two Poets Meet" 99

Lawrence Raab, "The Great Poem" 101

Betsy Retallack, "Roadside Special" 103

Liz Rosenberg, "The Other Woman's Point of View" 106

J. Allyn Rosser, "Discounting Lynn" 108

Kay Ryan, "Thin" 111

Mary Jo Salter, "A Phone Call to the Future" 112

Vijay Seshadri, "Memoir" 116

Alan Shapiro, "Misjudged Fly Ball" 117

Charles Simic, "House of Cards" 119

Gerald Stern, "Homesick"   120

James Tate, "The Loser"   122

Sue Ellen Thompson, "Body English"   124

Tony Towle, "Misprision"   126

Alison Townsend, "What I Never Told You About the Abortion"   128

Paul Violi, "Counterman"   131

Ellen Bryant Voigt, "Harvesting the Cows"   134

David Wagoner, "The Driver"   136

Charles Harper Webb, "Prayer to Tear the Sperm-Dam Down"   138

C. K. Williams, "Ponies"   141

Terence Winch, "Sex Elegy"   142

Susan Wood, "Gratification"   143

Franz Wright, "A Happy Thought"   145

Robert Wrigley, "Religion"   146

David Yezzi, "The Call"   147

Dean Young, "Clam Ode"   149

Contributors' Notes and Comments   151

Magazines Where the Poems Were First Published   189

Acknowledgments   193

David Lehman was born in New York City in 1948. He is the author of six books of poems, most recently *When a Woman Loves a Man* (Scribner, 2005). Among his nonfiction books are *The Last Avant-Garde: The Making of the New York School of Poets* (Anchor, 1999) and *The Perfect Murder* (Michigan, 2000). He edited the new edition of *The Oxford Book of American Poetry*, a one-volume comprehensive anthology of poems from Anne Bradstreet to the present. He also edited *Great American Prose Poems: From Poe to the Present*, which appeared from Scribner in 2003. He teaches writing and literature in the graduate writing program of the New School in New York City and offers an undergraduate course each fall on "Great Poems" at New York University. He initiated *The Best American Poetry* series in 1988 and received a Guggenheim Fellowship a year later. He lives in New York City and in Ithaca, New York.

FOREWORD

by David Lehman

◇ ◇ ◇

Back in 1992, when he made his first appearance in *The Best American Poetry*, Billy Collins was a little-known, hardworking poet who had won a National Poetry Series contest judged by Edward Hirsch. He had supported himself for many years by teaching English and was, like many other poets, looking for a publisher. Charles Simic chose "Nostalgia" from *The Georgia Review* for *The Best American Poetry 1992* and for the following year's *Best*, Louise Glück selected "Tuesday, June 4th, 1991" from *Poetry*. Others, too, recognized Collins's talent. The University of Pittsburgh Press began to publish his books in its estimable series directed by Ed Ochester. Radio host Garrison Keillor gave Collins perhaps the biggest boost of all by asking him to read his poems on the air. He did, and the audience loved what it heard. Collins grew popular. At the same time, it was understood that he was no less serious for having the common touch. Asked to explain his poetic lineage, he liked citing Coleridge's "conversation" poems, such as "This Lime-Tree Bower My Prison." And for all their genial whimsy, many of Collins's efforts have a decidedly literary flavor, with such subjects as "Tintern Abbey," Emily Dickinson, *The Norton Anthology of English Literature*, poetry readings, writing workshops, "Keats's handwriting," and Auden's "Musée des Beaux Arts." John Updike put it exactly when he described Collins's poems as "limpid, gently and consistently startling, more serious than they seem." In 2000, two publishers quarreled publicly over the rights to publish Collins's books, and the *New York Times* reported the story on page one. The unlikely success story reached its apogee a year after September 11, 2001, when Billy Collins read "The Names," a poem he had written for the somber occasion, to a rare joint session of Congress.

By then Collins had become a phenomenon. While remaining a member in good standing of the poetry guild, an entity with a purely notional existence whose members would theoretically starve for their art, he had regular contact with honest-to-goodness book-buying readers who were not themselves practicing poets. They numbered in the tens of thousands and made best-sellers of his books. He won a Guggenheim Fellowship and a grant from the National Endowment for the Arts. His poems were published in respected journals such as *The Atlantic* and *Poetry* and were chosen by the diverse quartet of John Hollander, Robert Bly, Rita Dove, and Robert Hass for four consecutive volumes of *The Best American Poetry*. In June 2001, Collins succeeded Stanley Kunitz as Poet Laureate of the United States, and I remember hearing people gripe about the appointment. Collins was regularly dismissed as an "easy" or "anecdotal" poet. It was then that I knew he had made it big. Harold Bloom has propounded the theory that poets fight Oedipal battles with ancestors of their choice, so that Wallace Stevens had to overcome Keats's influence as Wordsworth had earlier overcome Milton's. It sometimes seems to me that a different Freudian paradigm—sibling rivalry—may explain the behavior of contemporary poets, for the backbiting in our community is ferocious, and nothing signifies success better than ritual bad-mouthing by rivals or wannabes.

The story as I've sketched it broadly here illustrates more than one useful lesson. Probably the most important is that poetry has the potential to reach masses of people who read for pleasure, still and always the best reason for reading. Radio is a great resource for spreading the word, and attention from programs such as Keillor's *Writer's Almanac*, Terry Gross's *Fresh Air*, and the interview shows of Leonard Lopate in New York City and Michael Silverblatt in Los Angeles is among the best things that can happen to a book or an author. Another lesson is that some poets share a resistance to popularity—other people's popularity, above all—though they might bristle if you called them elitist. It's a problem that afflicts us all to some extent. We say we want real readers, who buy our books not as an act of charity but as a free choice, yet should one in our party escape the poetry ghetto, we tremble with ambivalence, as if having real readers means a sure loss in purity. Inevitably the discussion turns to a question that seems substantive. What accounts for an individual poet's popular appeal? Does popularity result from (or result in) a loss of artistic integrity? What makes the lucky one's star shine so bright that it can be seen to sparkle even in the muddy skies of the metropolis, where industrial wastes have all but abolished the sighting of a heavenly body?

To the second of these questions, the answer is a simple no. Collins's readers came to him; he did not alter his style or his seriousness to curry anyone's favor. (It is, in fact, entirely possible that the poet setting out to be the most popular on the block stands the least chance of achieving that goal.) The answer to the other questions begins with the surface of Collins's poems, which is amiable, likable, relaxed. Even critics of Collins would concede that his poems have a high quotient of charm. He is, to ring a variant on a theme from Wordsworth, unusually fluent in the language of an adult speaking to other adults in the vernacular. Moreover, he insists on the primacy of the ordinary, as when he expresses contentment in "an ordinary night at the kitchen table, / at ease in a box of floral wallpaper, / white cabinets full of glass, / the telephone silent, / a pen tilted back in my hand." I would wager that Collins's ability to find and express contentment in the ordinary has contributed in a major way to his popular appeal. Wit and humor, traits of his verse, don't hurt. Above all, his poems make themselves available to the mythical general reader that book publishers crave. You don't need to have been an English major to get a Collins poem such as "Osso Buco" or "Nightclub." Such poems insist on a poetic pleasure principle. They are, to use a charged word, *accessible*. "Billy Collins's poetry is widely accessible," said Librarian of Congress James Billington in June 2001. "He writes in an original way about all manner of ordinary things and situations with both humor and a surprising contemplative twist." Collins himself has reservations about *accessible*, a word that he says suggests ramps for "poetically handicapped people." He prefers *hospitable*. But there's no dodging *accessible*, and in the introduction to his anthology *180 More*, Collins granted that the quality denoted by the word was what he looked for in a poem. An "accessible" poem, he wrote, is one that is "easy to enter," in the sense that an apartment or a house may be welcoming. "Some poems talk to us; others want us to witness an act of literary experimentation," he wrote, declaring his preference for the former and arguing that pleasure in poetry—its paramount purpose, according to Wordsworth—demands clarity.

The opposition between clarity and difficulty, or between communication and experimentation, is happily not absolute. Nor can we take it for granted that any of these terms has a fixed meaning that all can agree on. Accessibility—as a term and, implicitly, as a value—has been attacked recently by Helen Vendler in *The New Republic*. " 'Accessibility' needs to be dropped from the American vocabulary of aesthetic judgment if we are not to appear fools in the eyes of the world," Vendler wrote in the context of defending John Ashbery, "with his resolve against statement bearing the burden of a poem." Yet it is of course conceivable, it is even perhaps inevitable, that a poem by John Ashbery should be among the seventy-five poems chosen by Billy Collins for *The Best American Poetry*

2006. And so it has happened. Abstract discussion is one thing, poetic creativity and intuition is another, and it takes the former a long time to catch up with the latter. Let the debates continue. The poets themselves will make their choices, but they will do so on the basis of poems loved rather than positions held, rebuffed, or discarded.

There may be a structural antagonism between poets and critics, but at its best, criticism can make better writers of us, link poetry to its readership, and help build a community. The work of explanation, evaluation, and elucidation is there to be done. Unfortunately, much contemporary criticism is singularly shrill, sometimes gratuitously belligerent, even spiteful. I wonder where the rage comes from. Is it to overcompensate for the widespread if erroneous perception of poets as a band of favor-trading blurbists forever patting one another on the back? Or is the explanation simply that it is and always has been easier to issue summary judgments than to grapple with new art? I wonder, too, whether young poets flocking to MFA programs or working on their first manuscripts know what they're in for. It sometimes seems to me that the fledgling poet is in the position of the secret agent in Somerset Maugham's *Ashenden*, who gets his marching orders from a superior known only by his initial. "There's just one thing I think you ought to know before you take on this job," R. says. "And don't forget it. If you do well you'll get no thanks and if you get into trouble you'll get no help."

Perhaps when we review the reviewers, we should put a higher value on moments of mirth, such as Thom Geier of *Entertainment Weekly* provided last year. Geier opined inventively that John Ashbery's "oeuvre is not unlike Paris Hilton's" but "much, much smarter." There is so much to admire in this formulation—the word "oeuvre" bumping against that fussy "not unlike," and the double "much"—that one feels like a killjoy pointing out the comic outrageousness of the comparison. In the same magazine Billy Collins was characterized as simultaneously the Oprah of poetry, "the best buggy-whip maker of the 21st century," poetry's answer to Jerry Seinfeld ("hilariously funny"), a "modern-day Robert Frost," and "like Rodney Dangerfield," a figure who "doesn't get much respect in some serious literary circles," in part because his work is, yes, "accessible." Well, whatever else he is, Billy Collins is a natural choice to edit this year's *Best American Poetry*, and he has crafted an anthology that demonstrates the vitality of American poetry and showcases poems of wit, charm, humor, eloquence, ingenuity, and comic invention.

Every year I screen hundreds of newspaper articles touching on poetry, and there are always one or two items that linger longer in the memory. Two last year stood above the rest. One was in the obituaries for Jerry Orbach, an actor as skillful playing a cop on *Law and Order* as singing a chorus in *Carousel*. It turned out that Orbach wrote hundreds of short poems to his wife. Some were read at his funeral. In contrast to this loving memory was the terse funereal report filed by Carlotta Gall in the *New York Times* on November 8, 2005: "Afghan Poet Dies After Beating by Husband." Nadia Anjuman, twenty-five, who had just published a book of poems—*Gule Dudi*, or "Dark Flower"—and had a second one ready for publication, had an argument with her husband. He beat her up, gave her a black eye, and knocked her unconscious; she died in the hospital. Five days later, Christina Lamb's article in the *Sunday Times* of London fleshed out the story. Nadia Anjuman was a woman of great courage as well as talent. In the city of Herat in western Afghanistan, she had joined a group that called itself the "Sewing Circles of Herat." Under this cover the women met, at the Golden Needle Sewing School, not to make clothes but to study literature and poetry in defiance of the Taliban's edicts forbidding women from studying. (The Taliban also forbade women to laugh out loud.) The women of the "Sewing Circles" risked grave penalties, imprisonment or worse, if caught. Nadja Anjuman survived these underground heroics but not, apparently, the wrath of a family that regarded as shameful the publication of a woman's poems about love and beauty. Brutally murdered, she left behind a six-month-old child and poems that continue to be read. "My wings are closed and I cannot fly," she laments in one ghazal, which concludes, "I am an Afghan woman, and must wail."

Was this tragic sequence of events a parable about the continuing plight of Afghani women four years after the defeat of the Taliban? An allegory in which the wielders of the pen suffer devastating losses before triumphing over the wielders of the sword? It may have been neither of these or other things that spring to mind. Yet I couldn't help translating the story into one in which poetry, emblem of free expression that it is, may be threatened with violent reprisal ending in death. Poetry, even the poetry of humor and delight, is an agent of the imagination pressing back, in Wallace Stevens's phrase, against the pressure of reality.

Billy Collins is the author of six books of poetry, including *Sailing Alone Around the Room* (2001), *Picnic, Lightning* (1997), *The Art of Drowning* (1995), *The Apple That Astonished Paris* (1988), and *Questions About Angels* (1991), which was selected by Edward Hirsch for the National Poetry Series. He also has recorded a spoken-word CD, *The Best Cigarette* (1997). He has received fellowships from the New York Foundation for the Arts, the National Endowment for the Arts, and the Guggenheim Foundation. He has also won the Bess Hokin Prize, the Frederick Bock Prize, the Oscar Blumenthal Prize, and the Levinson Prize—all awarded by *Poetry* magazine. In October 2004, Collins was the inaugural recipient of the Poetry Foundation's Mark Twain Award for humorous poetry. He has served as a Literary Lion of the New York Public Library and he is a distinguished professor of English at Lehman College, City University of New York, where he has taught for the past thirty years. He served as Poet Laureate of the United States from 2001 to 2003.

INTRODUCTION

by Billy Collins

◊   ◊   ◊

SEVENTY-FIVE NEEDLES
IN THE HAYSTACK OF POETRY

How many poems see the light of print in America each year? To find the answer simply multiply the number of literary magazines in the United States by the average number of poems per issue times the number of issues each year. That's right: too many. It's enough to make you wish the NEA would award grants to poets for not writing, like the ones farmers get for not growing crops. And partially because of this glut of publications, there is also a quality problem to be faced. A friend of mine announced one night over dinner that 83 percent of contemporary poetry is not worth reading. Somehow, that number, pulled out of the air, continues to seem deadly accurate. I should add quickly that I count myself among those whose lives would be sorely impoverished without the dependable availability of the remaining 17 percent. With those percentages in mind, what I have been doing among other things for the past year as guest editor of this volume is reading more contemporary poems than anyone should be expected to and sorting them roughly into two piles, one noticeably taller than the other. Literary judges typically complain about the difficulty of making up their minds when faced with such an abundance of good work, but I found it fairly easy to man the pearly gates of this annual collection. Poems either left me cold or caught me in their spell. Into the big pile went many poems I gave up on before I got to the end. Into the small pile went ones that held my attention, and when it came down to the harder final calls, the stayers were ones that invited me to return to their first lines again. And the reward for paging through 1,754 magazines—to pull another number out of the air—is this terrific group of seventy-five, which this book, true to form, has declared the year's "best."

Several past guest editors have felt a need to make apologies for that superlative. In these hypersensitive times when the lighting of a cigarette is regarded as a moral offense, why be surprised that the notion of ranking poems would be cause for discomfort? It might have something to do with a falsely elevated conception of what poetry is. Britain's Booker Prize is one of many handed out for fiction and attended by lively public gossip and often shameless declarations from the short-listed. But competitiveness and poetry do not seem to go together equally as well. Is it the putative sanctity of poetry, its post-Romantic veneration, that makes it, in the minds of some, immune from value judgments (how dare you!), claims of superiority (the nerve!), and discrimination (but what about the others?!)? Is poetry thought to occupy a realm beyond the grim reality of earthly competition? Or is there a baser cause? Have the loudest objectors been driven to such ill feeling by their perennial exclusion? Frankly, the designation "best" doesn't bother me. At worst, the title is a marketing strategy designed to encourage book sales and maybe convert some new readers to poetry. Who would reach for a book called *Some Fairly Decent Poems*? In one way, "best" meant I could simply pick what I liked, just as I had done when I put together a website and two anthologies in the "Poetry 180" program. *De gustibus non est disputandum*, yawned the recumbent Roman, or to alter Fran Lebowitz's unassailable definition of good and bad music, good poetry is poetry I like, and bad poetry is poetry I don't like. But I was always convinced that I could find enough very good poems to make an edition that would demonstrate the strength and imaginative diversity of the poetry being written in America today.

Admittedly, a more accurate but less catchy title for this collection would be "Best American Poetry According to the Skewed, Erratic Taste of the Present Editor." And since no one can—or would want to—read every single poem published in America for the year, "best" really means the best of the ones that happened to come my way. It is just possible that there are some not-so-mute but still inglorious Miltons out there whose work never found its way to me, but my wide reading indicated rather a preponderance of poems written by non-Miltons who might want to consider muteness as an alternative to poetry writing. Perhaps the low reputation of autocratic critical judgment is what makes people uncomfortable about literary selectivity. Surely, *judgmental* was not always a term of condemnation. With the notable exception of the shadow-casting figure of Harold Bloom, few of today's critics utter declarations about the value of literary works based solely on their own informed taste. For better or worse, the days of Eliot, Empson, and Jarrell are as gone as the snows of yesteryear. The confidence that emboldened such fearless critics gradually shriveled in the decades that witnessed the rise of theoretical criticism, whether of the Viennese or French variety. When personal taste was a legitimate basis for literary criticism, readers looked to critics to guide and deepen their literary experience by pointing them toward works of value and saving them from wasting time on dross. I admit to feeling nostalgic for those days. I generally find it easier to digest a statement such as "No other living poet has written so well about the actions of ordinary men" (Jarrell on Frost) than I do the syntactical thickets that mark contemporary critical discourse. Actually, I'm getting a little sick of the word *discourse*. (Do I sound irritable? There is a very noisy playground across from where I am writing.)

The case that competition harms poetry by commodifying it is a weak one given the realities of publication. Any time a poem is submitted to a journal, the poet enters a silent competition with all the writers whose work is on the desk of the poetry editor. To make matters worse, poems are often competing for the attention not of the editor but of a young, freshly empowered screener. The editor, of course, does what editors are paid to do: pick the best. Why would subscribers settle for less? Didn't the ads promise them "the very best in contemporary writing"? The same is true of manuscripts submitted to presses in the hope that books might come of them. This competitiveness is increasingly visible with the trend in university presses and small presses to ignore manuscripts unless they are sent as entries to a publication contest, the way horses are entries in a horse race. Such competitions take place not in the presence of spectators but behind the scenes, a covertness that makes the poetry slam, for all its hectoring and vulgarity, a kind of full disclosure of what is really going on in the literary marketplace.

For me, the thorny word in the title of this book is not *best* but *poetry*, because I am rarely sure of what we are talking about when we talk about poetry. Serious discussions of poetry commonly imply a very narrow definition of the genre. When I hear it said that "poetry . . . is about the extending of human consciousness, making conscious the unconscious, creating a symbolic consciousness that in its finest moments overcomes all the dualities in which the human world is cruelly and eternally . . . enmeshed," I wonder if that would include Alexander Pope's "Epistle to Dr. Arbuthnot" or the Yukon poems of Robert Service. When I read that "poetry's perpetual direction is its way of ensouling events, of seeking the doubleness in the events, the events' hidden or contradictory meaning," I get the feeling the writer did not have in mind Chaucer's ribaldry in "The Miller's Tale," Swift's vituperative "The Character of Sir Robert

Walpole," or Ovid's "The Art of Love," where advice on the bedding of women is happily offered. Can Catullus telling Minimus that his girlfriend is the cheapest whore in Rome be "ensouled"? So much poetry—traditional and contemporary—falls outside the circle of such discussions that we might pause in our awareness of how small an area is circumscribed by such high-sounding, presumptuous critical talk. Many vital poems are excluded for being too ludic, satirical, insufficiently hallowed, or for coming up short in the sensitivity department. But they are poetry, too. In fact, such a wild hodgepodge of verbal activity takes place under the heading "poetry" that the term has been stretched beyond its ability to be defined. Can Ogden Nash and Paul Verlaine be expected to sleep soundly in the same bed?

Now a word about the skewed, erratic taste of this editor. In burrowing through stacks of magazines, I went by poem, not by author's name. I am happy to report that I had never heard of roughly a third of the seventy-five chosen poets—a result, no doubt, of my ignorance, not their lack of reputation. When I say I read well over a thousand poems during the course of the year, I really mean that I started to read well over a thousand poems. In many cases, something stopped me from finishing or I rushed to the end just to make sure nothing surprising was going to happen. Often, I failed to hear a human voice speaking to me. Too many poems seemed oblivious to my presence and not the least interested in my participation as a reader. If you're not going to talk to me, then I'm going to stop listening, I would grumble as I turned the page. I also looked for and often did not find a sense of manifest content, a degree of surface clarity. When I begin reading a poem (call me crazy) I am looking for coordinates that will orient me by giving me somewhere to stand—a place to cross the border, a point of entry. I am bored by poems that are transparent from beginning to end, but I am quick to put down poems whose opening lines make me feel I have walked in on the middle of a Swedish movie being run backward with no subtitles.

But just because a poem is reasonably intelligible doesn't mean it's worth reading. When John Ciardi was poetry editor of *The Saturday Review*, he published a list of immediate deal-breakers, flaws that prevented him from reading any further and thus allowed him to devote more time to the search for good work; the mention of mythological beings and the apostrophe "Oh!" found places on his list. I have a few of my own. The word *cicada*, for example, stops me in my tracks. Sorry. I simply cannot continue. Poems consisting largely of memories tend to leave me unfurled, particularly memories of family members—parents, grandparents, especially ones referred to as "Dad," "Mom," "Grandpa," and "Grannie." The same goes for poems that seem obsessed with some object associated with a dead person: Grandpa's toolbox, Mom's ironing board, Dad's fishing rod, and the like. I was surprised to see how much poetic room such necro-fetishes are taking up these days. Poems brimming with personal nostalgia were easy to put aside. Some key words here are "Chevy," "we used to," "screen door," "the old Motorola," and, again, "Dad" himself. I also turned quickly away from poems that presumed an interest on my part in the poet-speaker's psychic condition (usually misery) while showing no interest in providing any degree of linguistic pleasure, which, according to Coleridge, is the "immediate object of poetry." Too many poems seemed content to convey an experience followed by a reaction to it without factoring in the reader's presumed indifference to the inner lives of strangers. Open enrollment in this perception/reaction school began with the "loco-descriptive" poems of the late eighteenth century. Such poems typically begin by presenting a speaker fixed in a landscape. The speaker describes his natural surroundings then falls into a reverie, returning at the end of the poem to the original scene, which now appears altered by the intervening shifts in the speaker's consciousness. The most distilled example of an "I-came-I saw-I-felt" poem might be Wordsworth's "I Wandered Lonely as a Cloud," commonly known as the "daffodil poem." I saw a lot of daffodils, the poet tells us—no, really, tons of them—and whenever I think back on that day I feel . . . exuberant! "Who cares?" would have been a legitimate response at the time of the poem's composition, because the presumptuousness of the Romantic show-and-tell method had not yet established itself as the new content of poetry. Today, its position as the dominant type seems secure. But if a poet is incapable of pleasing the reader with verbal and imaginative thrills, is it really enough for him to write that he saw something (the stars in the sky) and that it made him feel something (rather small)?

So what makes one poem better than another? Harold Bloom thinks that the question is "more crucial today than ever before, since extrapoetic considerations of race, ethnicity, gender, sexual orientation, and assorted ideologies increasingly constitute the grounds for judgment in the educational institutions and the media of the English-speaking world." To shine a more positive light on the subject, let me attempt to say what it is about certain poems that widened my eyes. The recognizable sound of a human voice is always an inducement to continue. I prefer to act as an auditor rather than a witness to an act of literary alchemy.

I was also made alert by poems that appeared to be going somewhere, poems that were taking me on an imaginative journey. I was drawn to poems where the poet did not seem completely sure of where he or she was headed. Emerson compared writing to ice skating in that the writer might be taken places he did not intend to go. And Formula 1 driver Mario Andretti once said, "If you feel that everything is under control, you're just not driving fast enough." Obviously, to go somewhere, you have to start somewhere. Being oriented at the outset of a poem offers the promise of being pleasantly disoriented later as the poem moves into more complex territory where the waters are more strangely stirred. Highly explicit titles can orient the reader precisely: "Lines Written on a Wayside Bench in Spring" or "Elegy for the Duke of Grafton Burned to Death in his Bugatti at the Limerick Grand Prix." But opening lines are where readers usually look for their bearings. A poem that starts in the "factual" ("I am looking out the kitchen window" or "I am sitting on a flagpole") can move from that starting place into more nebulous areas. This kind of progression from clarity to mystery, this gradual deepening, has long characterized the movement of the lyric poem. Once in a poetry class (an elementary one), a student asked me what those tiny numbers were doing alongside the poem we were reading. After I explained that they were line numbers, I added that they were also like the numbers on the sides of swimming pools indicating depth. The poem gets deeper as it goes along; and it has a better chance of doing that if it starts out in the shallow end, I went on, kicking the metaphor up and down the aisles.

The stakes seem lower to me in static poems where the poet is content to decorate a memory, "poeticize" an experience, or simply indulge in the folly of "self-expression." Poems with a sense of journey gave the impression that the poet was figuring out the direction of the poem as it went along. My attention quickened when I heard in a poem "the sound of thinking," as James Longenbach puts it, "not the sound of finished thought but the sound of a mind alive in the syntactical process of discovering what it might be thinking." Poems act more alive and immediate when they exhibit a degree of self-awareness by turning on themselves or commenting on their own existence. The poem then becomes the event itself, not just the report of a past experience. Perhaps the very best poems combine an acute awareness of tradition with a unique freshness of voice. The result of this double accomplishment may be a tone of playful irreverence; the past cannot be mocked unless it is known and therefore acknowledged. I was drawn to poets who clearly had not had the high school beaten out of them by college—pranksters and mischief makers who are testing the last remains of poetic decorum. Megan Gannon's "List of First Lines," Joy Katz's "Just a second ago," and wiseguy Mark Pawlak's "The Sharper the Berry" are striking examples. In the end, I read as any hedonist would and found my pleasures wherever I could.

If you are anything like me, you do not turn to poetry because you are interested in the author; you go there because you are interested in yourself and you see poetry as a means of stimulating your sense of being. If you are a poet, you read other poets for inspiration, that is, for opportunities to steal, or for the possibility that another poet will open a door for you that you never knew existed. But the primary reason for reading is pleasure, and, dry as it sounds to say so, the primary source of poetic pleasure is form. The content of a poem may be personal to the point of narcissism, self-involved to the point of autism, but its form—that is, any feature that gives the poem cohesion and keeps it from drifting into chaos—is communal, inclusive, even cordial.

Among these seventy-five poems, there are both inherited forms and ad hoc patternings. There are sonnets by Paul Muldoon and Marilyn Nelson, prose poems by Daniel Gustein and James Tate, a sort of ode by Dean Young, a Laura Cronk sestina, plenty of couplets, tercets, and quatrains, and even a sequence of limericks by R. S. Gwynn. More improvised or homemade forms guide Kim Addonizio's series of subverted adages, Julie Larios's double abecedarian, and the near stichomythia of Paul Violi's "Counterman." But whether a poem is casually patterned or set in the locked and fully upright position, it can be said that all good poetry is formal poetry. Even the least formally attired poem, if mindfully composed, will set up "frameworks of expectation," in John Hollander's words. Such poems carry us forward through a series of steps that lead—or ironically fail to lead—to some revelation, a notion, or even an angle of vision that was not possible before that poem was written. The way of the poem takes us to a place that did not exist before the poem was written. A poem is the path of its own going and the only access to its ending. And besides the rhythm of the line, which sometimes can be scanned and identified, there is the less obvious rhythm of the whole poem, the pacing of its parts, the gradual release of its energy, its rhetorical pulsations. Whether traditional or invented, form is a guide that provides the poet with a condition under which to write, thus avoiding mere tantrum. And once established, form holds the reader in its embrace. Form finally gives proof that the poem is the result of a negotiation between the poet and an essentially uncooperative language. Many poems included here can claim as their form simply their sense of journeying, the steady movement that points toward the destination of the final lines, the unfolding path of a poem's progress. These more loosely constructed poems—see Bao Phi's "Race" and Mark Halliday's "Refusal to Notice Beautiful Women"—must be seen as examples of a now dominant type, which has meant the untuning of traditionally regulated poetry.

Once Walt Whitman demonstrated that poetry in English could get along without standard meter and end-rhyme, poetry began to lose that familiar gait and musical jauntiness that listeners and readers had come to identify with it. But poetry also lost something more: a trust system that had bound poet and reader together through the reliable recurrence of similar sounds and a steady dependable beat. Whatever emotional or intellectual demands a poem placed on the reader, at least the reader could put trust in the poet's implicit promise to keep up a tempo and maintain a sound pattern. It's the same promise that is made to the listeners of popular songs. What has come to replace this system of trust, if anything? However vague a substitute, the answer is probably tone of voice. As a reader, I come to trust or distrust the authority of the poem after reading just a few lines. Do I hear a voice that is making reasonable claims for itself—usually a first-person voice speaking fallibly but honestly—or does the poem begin with a grandiose pronouncement, a riddle, or an intimate confession foisted on me by a stranger? Tone may be the most elusive aspect of written language, but our ears instantly recognize words that sound authentic and words that ring false. The character of the speaker's voice played an indescribable but essential role in the making of those two piles I mentioned, one much taller than the other.

So welcome, readers, to a plurality of poets, a cornucopia of tropes, and a range of interests. Herein lies an apology to a bird (Gaylord Brewer), a mock grammar (Tom Christopher), an epithalamion (Laura Cronk), motherly advice (Denise Duhamel), a close encounter with a mermaid (Debora Greger), a study in comparative religions (R. S. Gwynn), a solution to the problem of beautiful women (Mark Halliday), a ferry ride (Katia Kapovich), a visit to a Civil War battlefield (Laura Kasischke), a police chase (Mark Kraushaar), a slew of insults (Mark Pawlak), a bank heist (David Wagoner), and a full-blown drag race (Bao Phi).

As with any anthology, you can dip in anywhere. The order is alphabetical, as usual, so the sequence is left to Dame Fortune, who has wiles of her own. Thanks to her, Lawrence Raab gets to walk arm in arm with

Betsy Retallack, Charles Harper Webb can rub elbows with C. K. Williams, and Alison Townsend has the pleasure of sitting between a couple of witty old friends, Tony Towle and Paul Violi. The authors' notes, a prominent feature of this series, invite one to flip back and forth from poem to comment. Being taken backstage like that can be revealing, but don't be surprised if the two sometimes don't seem to match. Poets are notoriously unreliable commentators on their own work, as they should be. Getting a poet to talk about his or her poem is like trying to get a dog to look into a mirror; no matter how well-groomed the poodle, these creatures prefer the smell of something real to their own scentless reflections. A lesson for us all.

Finally, thanks are due to David Lehman for trusting my judgment and generously facilitating the process of selection. Thanks also to the astute George Green for drawing my attention to poems I might have otherwise overlooked, and to Kathy Ossip, who provided indispensable assistance. And thanks, of course, to the seventy-five poets gathered here for providing me (and now lots of others) with such a rich assortment of pleasures.

THE
BEST
AMERICAN
POETRY
2006

◇   ◇   ◇

Verities

◇   ◇   ◇

Into every life a little ax must fall.
Every dog has its choke chain.
Every cloud has a shadow.
Better dead than fed.
He who laughs, will not last.
Sticks and stones will break you,
and then the names of things will be changed.
A stitch in time saves no one.
The darkest hour comes.

from *Poetry*

DICK ALLEN

"See the Pyramids Along the Nile"

◊　◊　◊

I'll not be doing that now, nor the tropical islands,
the Algerian marketplace, the sunrise, the ocean.
Too many years vanished. I'll be in a cottage by a lake,
stumbling through books with pages missing,
looking from doorways at my nondescript backyard.
But Godspeed those who still wander,
Godspeed the great lovers, the great adventurers,
the movies and statues they'll become,
lonesome and blue. . . . Here, this evening,
everything will be quiet except my neighbor's buzz-saw
cutting into even lengths the wood
he'll use for something or other that he doesn't need . . .
and all I didn't do or dare to do
will haunt me—those dreams appearing elsewhere,
the jungle wet with rain,
you who I never met, arms lifted up into another's arms,
in a small house in Cairo, in a market stall
with the abacus and the veils,
or three rows ahead, your face tucked toward the window,
when I belonged to no one on that silver plane.

from *Boulevard*

CRAIG ARNOLD

from *Couple from Hell*

◊ ◊ ◊

11

You walk out in the morning
    and the sky is broad and blue,
and across the pathway threads of silk
    glint in the sun—at the end of each a spider,
still wet from the egg, spins out a dragline
    and sails off into the breeze.
The air is so bright and busy
    your whole body feels it,
a puppet weightless on its wires,
    and you let yourself be guided down the path
you've never dared to take, along the river,
    the little harbor at its mouth
where three blue boats are moored
    at a dock cushioned with old tires,
where the only sound is the deep bass
    drumming of waves on wood.

Here is a small café
    opening for breakfast,
a zinc counter catching the light
    at every angle in bright rings of glitter.
A cup of black coffee is placed before you,
    brimming with rainbow-colored foam,
a packet of sugar, a pat of butter,
    a split roll of bread
scored and toasted and still warm.
    The butter is just soft enough to spread,

the coffee hot and sugared to perfect sweetness,
    the bread grilled to the palest brown,
crisp, but not quite dry—
    you tear it neatly into pieces
and eat them slowly, and when you finish
    you are exactly full.

Here are bread, butter, and coffee.
    Here you are, your own body,
eating and drinking what you are given,
    as one day you in turn will be devoured,
and that is all. You were never the lord
    of a lightless kingdom, any more
than she has ever been its queen,
    and the world you talked each other into prison
suddenly seems to be made of glass,
    and your eyes see clear to the horizon,
and you feel the molecules of air
    part like a curtain, as if to let you pass.

from *Barrow Street*

A Worldly Country

◇   ◇   ◇

Not the smoothness, not the insane clocks on the square,
the scent of manure in the municipal parterre,
not the fabrics, the sullen mockery of Tweety Bird,
not the fresh troops that needed freshening up. If it occurred
in real time, it was O.K., and if it was time in a novel
that was O.K., too. From palace and hovel
the great parade flooded avenue and byway
and turnip fields became just another highway.
Leftover bonbons were thrown to the chickens
and geese, who squawked like the very dickens.
There was no peace in the bathroom, none in the china closet
or the banks, where no one came to make a deposit.
In short all hell broke loose that wide afternoon.
By evening all was calm again. A crescent moon
hung in the sky like a parrot on its perch.
Departing guests smiled and called, "See you in church!"
For night, as usual, knew what it was doing,
providing sleep to offset the great ungluing
that tomorrow again would surely bring.
As I gazed at the quiet rubble, one thing
puzzled me: What had happened, and why?
One minute we were up to our necks in rebelliousness,
and the next, peace had subdued the ranks of hellishness.

So often it happens that the time we turn around in
soon becomes the shoal our pathetic skiff will run aground in,

And just as waves are anchored to the bottom of the sea
we must reach the shallows before God cuts us free.

from *The New Yorker*

Speech in a Chamber

◇   ◇   ◇

In this book birds are taught their flying
by that which would make them fall
were they not to fly as had been taught.

The book is roughly bound, and left
open on a couch. The page is illustrated
and, lifted to the light, displays

a moralizing scene: two children have tied
a third to the wheel of an enormous carriage.
A group of elderly women look on with pride.

It is a scent of such astonishing strength,
why, Leopold, there are flowers hidden
throughout the room. There must be for I

cannot sleep without the noise of a bouquet,
and gently, gently, sir, you know
I sleep most gently in this small room.

from *The Paris Review*

Letter
from My Ancestors

◊   ◊   ◊

We wouldn't write this,
wouldn't even think of it. We are working
people without time on our hands. In the old country,

we milk cows or deliver the mail or leave,
scattering to South Africa, Connecticut, Missouri,
and finally, California for the Gold Rush—

Aaron and Lena run the Yosemite campground, general
store, a section of the stagecoach line. Morris comes
later, after the earthquake, finds two irons

and a board in the rubble of San Francisco.
Plenty of prostitutes need their dresses pressed, enough
to earn him the cash to open a haberdashery and marry

Sadie—we all have stories, yes, but we're not thinking
stories. We have work to do, and a dozen children. They'll
go on to pound nails and write up deals, not musings.

We document transactions. Our diaries record
temperatures, landmarks, symptoms. We
do not write our dreams. We place another order,

make the next delivery, save the next
dollar, give another generation—you,
maybe—the luxury of time

to write about us.

from *Margie*

You Must Have Been a Beautiful Baby

◊   ◊   ◊

Lenny Schlossberg, with a wonderful musical voice,
    applauded several other acts in the talent show—

A little girl doing a dance routine, an old woman playing
    an unrecognizable piece by Brahms on the grand piano onstage,
    and one or two others—

"She's ter-rific!" he said about the little girl, and about
    the old woman he said, "She's ter-rific!"

After singing three songs, which concluded the show,
    Lenny came back to my table with a smile and a Certificate
    of Appreciation.

"I love my name!" he said, showing it to me
    on the certificate. "Lenny Schlossberg!"

"It's a great name," I agreed. "It should be in lights."
    "Would you believe it? I've never had an argument
    with anybody," he said.

"I was in the air force in World War Two. I was in England, carrying
    messages. I made eighty flights and I never once had an argument!"

These were the songs that Lenny Schlossberg sang: "How Deep
   Is the Ocean," "I've Grown Accustomed to Her Face," and—
   for the director of the program,

The one who handed him his Certificate of Appreciation—
   "You Must Have Been a Beautiful Baby."

from *Fulcrum*

Apologia
to the Blue Tit

◇   ◇   ◇

We rise, drop our faces
in cold water, and face the prospects
of a day like the last one from which we
have not recovered.
                    —Philip Levine

Your preposterous death I contained
entirely in my palm, gave meaning
that meant nothing. Your name no longer
tolerated humor. My hand trembled,
the arm, the body itself from the folds
of its nightly deviations. Soft lemon
of breast no wider than a fingertip.
Each dead wing I lifted and let drop.
Uncurled small talons, let grip air again.
You were still warm with a memory
of life, it occurred to me, and I held
your head—your azure cap, the dark line
of broken nape—carefully in a crucible
of bone and flesh, tendon, blood.
When a car turned down the long drive,
stuttering, gray, operated by a stranger,
why did I lower you in embarrassment,
study a sky promising plenty more trouble.
Why nod a greeting I didn't believe,
caught red-handed in my inspection

of beauty discarded and already rotting.
I laid you in a shaded knot of pine,
spears of cut grass as your pyre,
resumed the timely errands of the day.

from *The Briar Cliff Review* and *River Styx*

Rhetorical Figures

◇ ◇ ◇

When a sentence is composed of two independent
clauses, the second being weaker than the first,
it is called *One-Legged Man Standing*. If it
purposefully obscures meaning, it's called *Ring
Dropped in Muddy Creek*, or if elegantly composed,
Wasp Fucking Orchid. There are words behind words,
and half the time our thoughts spraying out like water
from a hose, half the time banging inside our heads
like a wren in a house. When a sentence ends
unexpectedly because someone has punched
the speaker in the face, it's *Avalanche Sudden*.
When instead the speaker is stopped with sloppy
kisses, it's *Dripping Cloud*. Not to be confused
with *Dripping Cone*, when someone overturns
the table, or *Bird Pecking the Mountain*, when
the sentence goes on for an hour and a half and ends
in a shaking death. If the speaker lies in the driveway
so drunk on cheap wine that one listening cannot
get close to the meaning and thus runs away again,
claiming, "For the last time," it's *Pregnant Dog
Cooked in Sun*. If the speaker sells everything for
an old convertible and drives out into the desert
with unintelligible shouting to the pissed-off stars:
Aching Stones Laughing. Forced incongruent words
are *Fishes on Fire*, and are beautiful but bring us
no closer to the Truth or the Cosmos or the All,
so either we tour Europe looking for the bodies
of saints or drink all night playing Johnny Cash LPs.
Everything we have said, we have said all our lives.

Same for what we haven't said. Learning the terms
doesn't help, we're still filled over the rim with longing.
Already in this poem there is *Clamshell Moon, Barn
House Burning, Cow Lowing the Field, One Hundred
Village Bells, Moth Flurry*. Somewhere above, a *Torn
Shirt*, a *Peasant Girl Crying*, a *Baby Dropped Through
Smoke to Voices Shouting*. Not much further a *Cat
in Heat*, a *Wailing Street*, and in the end *Tree Frogs
Blazing Reeds with Sound*.

from *Hayden's Ferry Review*

Sestina
for the Newly Married

◇   ◇   ◇

I just found out that my new husband
May have never married me at all
Had I been born with six digits on both feet.
Had I a deformity, he may have never looked my way.
My small irregularities didn't pose a problem,
And so here I sit, at work, married, writing a sestina.

A man can't help who he's attracted to, said Tina,
Spoken like a man herself or like my husband,
Who feels a man's attraction's not a problem.
There's no convincing, it just exists, that's all.
No court of friends and their persuasions can sway
A man sure of libido, sure of foot.

Swift of affection, swift of foot,
My husband felt the grand swelling of a Seguidilla,
That Spanish dance, intoxicating in its way.
It's the feeling that can make a man a husband.
Happily it brought him to me, handsome and tall,
Stepping so sweetly, the world lost all its problems.

Or I thought the world had lost its problems.
As I was being swept off my feet,
I forgot about other obligations, work and all.
The world was at war, which is a whole other sestina,
And there I was dancing and wooing with my could-be husband.
Crooning and mooning the world away.

Now it's done and we're here to stay.
Irregularities and all, attraction's not a problem.
Looking out with new eyes as wife and husband,
Still doe-eyed a bit, surveying the work at hand:
Thank-you notes to write, letters to our senators, sestinas,
Plays about the good life, mysteries, and that's not all.

We're beginning at the beginning, with so much to be done, it's all
Two people can do. In between the pitch and sway
Of our affections, the lovely gusts that sustain us,
There are promises, obligations to the problems
We put off. We're holding hands and stepping off feet
First into the water in our funny suits, a woman and her husband.

There really isn't sestina enough at all
To hold the feelings between a new wife and husband. To weigh
This love or display it is a problem. The words we have aren't quite fit.

from *LIT*

Our Generation

◊ ◊ ◊

Whatever they say about us, they have to agree
We managed to bridge the gap between
Those who arrived before us and those who've followed.
We learned enough at the schools available
To fill the entry-level positions at the extant sawmills
Our elders managed, at banks, freight yards, and hospitals,
Then worked our way up to positions of trust.
There we were, down on the shop floor
Or up in the manager's office, or outside the office
On scaffolds, washing the windows.
Did we work with joy? With no less joy
Than people felt in the generations before us.
And on weekends and weekday evenings
We did our best to pursue the happiness
Our founders encouraged us to pursue,
And with equal gusto. Whatever they say about us,
They can't deny that we filled the concert halls,
Movie houses, malls, and late-night restaurants.
We took our bows onstage or waited on tables
Or manned the refreshment booths to earn a little extra
For the things we wanted, the very things
Pursued by the generations before us
And likely to be pursued by generations to come:
Children and lawns and cars and beach towels.
And now and then we stood back to admire
The colorful spectacle, the endless variety,
As others before us admired it, and then returned
To fill our picnic baskets, drive to the park,
And use the baseball diamonds just as their makers

Intended they should be used. And if we too
Crowded into the square to cheer the officials
Who proclaimed our country as fine in fact
As it is in theory, a few of us, confined to a side street,
Carried signs declaring a truth less fanciful.
A few unheeded, it's true, but no more unheeded
Than a similar few in generations before us
Who hoped that the truth in generations to come,
Though just as homely, would find more followers.

from *The Kenyon Review*

Toward Some Bright Moment

◇   ◇   ◇

Was she drunk? She didn't seem drunk, had only
staggered a little, stumbling over the curb—
a blind woman on the corner of Broadway and Fourth,
kicking her dog, a mutt German shepherd, missing

half the time, and then hitting with a hollow thud,
and shouting, You fuck, and You dumb shit, over
and over. A gray day in March, slush in the streets,
a slight drizzle, a Saturday and the sidewalks packed.

You fuck, yanking the dog and kicking, a woman,
in her thirties, her face too twisted with anger
to tell if she was pretty or not; the dog abject
and cringing. No one stopped her, no one said,

You shouldn't do that, and I didn't either, people
giving her a wide berth, perhaps thinking, as I did,
that they couldn't know her pain, that being blind
gave her permission, that her stoicism had at last

collapsed, and wouldn't it collapse for us too,
those of us who could see? But there was the dog
crouched down, attempting to make itself smaller,
with an almost human expression of misery,

but not whining, just waiting for it to be over.
I wanted to cross the street and hit the woman,
knock her down, and I was shocked by this, as if
I'd done something equally wrong; but as she kept

kicking the dog so I wanted to kick her, so angry
did I become, because she didn't stop. In the time
it took me to draw near, slow down, and then pass on,
she kept up her assault, and even with my back turned

I still heard her shouts, while I kept telling myself
how all these other men and women on the street
also saw and heard her. They did as I did. I wasn't alone.
We were all righteous or culpable or comfortable

together. We all passed on, or at least until I had gone,
because I don't know what happened, if she stopped
on her own or if a cop stopped her or someone else
just couldn't bear it anymore. How often this image

comes back to me when I'm depressed or hate myself
or want to be better. I think what I might have done—
rescued the dog, led the woman away—though now
twelve years have passed. Even a certain kind of day

will bring it back, a wet city street, crowds of people
pushing toward some bright moment, the one to make
their lives complete—the wail of a car alarm, a tangle
of yellow cabs, a pigeon in the gutter crushed by a bus.

from *American Poetry Review*

"Please Don't Sit Like a Frog, Sit Like a Queen"

◇ ◇ ◇

*—graffiti inside the cubicle of a ladies' bathroom in a
university in the Philippines*

Remember to pamper, remember to preen.
The world doesn't reward a pimply girl.
Don't sit like a frog, sit like a queen.

Buy a shampoo that gives your locks sheen.
If your hair is straight, get it curled.
Remember to pamper, remember to preen.

Keep your breath minty and your teeth white and clean.
Paint your nails so they glisten, ten pearls.
Don't sit like a frog, sit like a queen.

Smile, especially when you're feeling mean.
Keep your top down when your take your car for a whirl.
Remember to pamper, remember to preen.

Don't give in to cravings, you need to stay lean
so you can lift up your skirt as you prance and twirl.
Don't sit like a frog, sit like a queen.

Don't marry the professor, marry the dean.
Marry the king, don't marry the earl.

Remember to pamper, remember to preen.
Don't sit like a frog, sit like a queen.

from *Columbia Poetry Review*

The Land of Is

◇   ◇   ◇

The woman whose backpack I helped lift
to the baggage rack in that suddenly sweet
compartment of a train was an art historian
from Marseilles. We talked Giotto
all the way to Naples, and fell asleep
in each other's arms.

Or was this an episode partially lived,
partially dreamed?

After my old Ford broke down in Yellowstone,
those grizzlies I invented, especially the one
standing upright near her cubs
as if declaring *no pasaran*—that story
has just the right feel.
Trust me. Even the Spanish belongs.

With that bar fight in Elko, however,
there's much still to solve. Should he be Mexican
because he was Mexican? And when,
exactly, should he pull his knife?
I keep changing my mind, sure only
of the scar on my arm—the importance
of mentioning it, I mean.

It's clear that a story not tilted
will rarely stand up. But sometimes

I find myself in the land of is, helpless
before the tyranny of this
or that sufficient thing.
That large wooden horse, for example,
with car parts for a head—the one
that silhouettes my property's edge—

I admit I placed it there, and love at dusk
to see the blackbirds ride its back
and the field of barley it overlooks
turn dark purple as night descends.

Strange horse, it is what it is,
all funk and fact, in a beautiful spot.
What could be worse?
I can't muster the slightest impulse
to make it rear up, or run amok.

from *The Georgia Review*

Souvenir

◇　◇　◇

Though we vacationed in a castle, though I
rode you hard one morning to the hum
of bees that buggered lavender, and later
we shared gelato by a spotlit dome
where pigeons looped like coins from a parade—
we weren't transported back to newlyweds.
We only had a week, between new jobs,
we both were pinched with guilt at leaving Claire.
When, in our most expensive, most romantic meal,
you laid your sunburned hand upon your heart,
it was just to check the phone was on.

When the trip was good as over—when the train
would take us overnight to Rome, the flight
would take us home—I had the unimportant
moment I keep having. I wonder if
we choose what we recall?
                                           The train
was unromantic, smoky. We found a free
compartment, claimed the two bench seats, and eyed
the door. Italians who peered in and saw
your shoes, my auburn hair, our *Let's Go: Rome*,
soon found another car. And we were glad.
But then, reluctantly, two couples entered,
settled suitcases on laddered racks,
exchanged some cautious greetings, chose their spots.
Then each one turned to snacks and magazines.
The miles scrolled by like film into its shell.
Night fell. Each took a toothbrush down the hall.

Returned. Murmured to the one he knew.
The man beside the window pulled the shade.
We each snapped off our light, slunk down until
our kneecaps almost brushed. And shut our eyes.

Entwined I found us, waking in the dark.
Our dozen interwoven knees, when jostled,
swayed, corrected, swayed the other way.
Knuckles of praying hands were what they seemed.
Or trees in old-growth forests, familiarly
enmeshed, one mass beneath the night wind's breath.
Or death, if we are good, flesh among flesh,
without self-consciousness, for once.
                                        Husband,
five years husband, you slept, our fellow travelers
slept, scuttling through black space and blacker time.
As we neared the lighted station, I closed my eyes.
Had I been caught awake, I would have moved.

from *Shenandoah*

27

List of First Lines

◇   ◇   ◇

when the winter sits as if

when a wrist gives

when you pour two saucersful for

when the sifter sticks

when the window

when drifts

when fenced in, staked down, full of forgetting, bent and kissed

when, if, then

when

when spoons tarnish

when the moon removes

when, whose

when wither isn't it—more drift, almost ash,

when half the calving's risked for fuller hands

when kindling's stacked, a packed pyramid—first fourteen, then thirteen inside when itching rends a loose stitch, a stray

when the wash creaks in a cold key on the line

when to burn

when to cut what won't brown, tie two ends, haul and hold

when water seals stone to sediment, stem to picture turns

when the kettle seethes a stream on warming hands

when the birds

when rooms split light like a bent tin

when the cabinet's stacked, still damp or dripping, isn't it evening

when seed scatters, buckshot-strewn, through, or threw with, this

when shadows, parceled out from edge to edge

when by the bed the loose green is gotten

when skin

when burns raw red instead of, still

when lying quiet

when told to turn

when sighing through a reed of barbed trees, try

from *Third Coast*

For My Niece Sidney, Age Six

◇ ◇ ◇

Did you know that boiling to death
was once a common punishment
in England and parts of Europe?
It's true. In 1542 Margaret Davy,
a servant, was boiled for poisoning
her employer. So says the encyclopedia.
That's the way I like to start my day:
drinking hot black coffee and reading
the 1910 *Encyclopedia Britannica*.
Its pages are tissue thin and the covers
rub off on your hands in dirt colored
crumbs (the kind a rubber eraser
makes) but the prose voice is all knowing
and incurably sure of itself. My 1956
World Book runs to 18 volumes and has red
pebbly covers. It begins at "Aardvark"
and ends with "Zygote." I used to believe
you could learn everything you'd ever
need by reading encyclopedias. Who
was E. B. Browning? How many Buddhists
in Burma? What is Byzantine art? Where
do bluebells grow? These days, I own five
sets of encyclopedias from various
eras. None of them ever breathed
a word about the fact that this humming,
aromatic, acid flashback, pungent, tingly
fingered world is acted out differently

for each one of us by the puppet theatre
of our senses. Some of us grow up doing
credible impressions of model citizens
(though sooner or later hairline
cracks appear in our façades). The rest
get dubbed eccentrics, unnerved and undone
by other people's company, for which we
nevertheless pine. Curses, outbursts
and distracting chants simmer all day
long in the Crock-Pots of our heads.
Encyclopedias contain no helpful entries
on conducting life's business while the ruckus
in your skull keeps competing for your
attention; or on the tyranny of the word
normal—its merciless sway over those
of us bedeviled and obsessed,
hopeless at school dances, repelled by
mothers' suffocating hugs, yet entranced
by foul-smelling chemistry experiments,
or eager to pass sleepless nights seeking
rhymes for *misspent* and *grimace*.
Dear girl, your jolly blond one-year-old
brother, who adults adore, fits into
the happy category of souls mostly at home
in the world. He tosses a fully clothed doll
into the inflatable wading pool in your
backyard *(splash!)* and laughs maniacally
at his own comic genius. You sit alone,
twenty feet from everyone else, on a stone
bench under a commodious oak, reading aloud,
gripping your book like the steering wheel
of a race car you're learning to drive.
Complaints about you are already filtering
in. You're not big on eye contact or smiling.
You prefer to play by yourself. You pitch fits.
Last week you refused to cut out and paste
paper shapes with the rest of the kids.
You told the kindergarten teacher you were
going to howl like a wolf instead, which you did
till they hauled you off to the principal's

31

office. Ah, the undomesticated smell
of open rebellion! Your troublesome legacy,
and maybe part of your charm, is to shine
too hotly and brightly at times, to be lost
in the maze of your sensations, to have
trouble switching gears, to be socially
clueless, to love books as living things,
and therefore to be much alone. If you like,
when I die, I'll leave you my encyclopedias.
They're wonderful company. Watching you
read aloud in your father's garden, as if
declaiming a sermon for hedges, I recall
reading about Martin Luther this morning.
A religious reformer born in 1483, he nailed
his grievances, all 95 of them, to a German
church door. Fiery, impossible, untamable
girl, I bet you too post your grievances
in a prominent place someday. Anyway,
back to boiling. The encyclopedia says
the worst offenders were "boiled without
benefit of clergy," which I guess means
they were denied the right to speak
to a priest before being lowered into scalding
water and cooked like beets. Martin Luther
believed we human beings contain the "inpoured
grace of god," as though grace were lemonade,
and we are tumblers brim full of it. Is grace
what we hold in without spilling a drop,
or is it an outflooding, a gush of messy
befuddling loves? The encyclopedia never
explains *why* Margaret Davy poisoned her employer,
what harm he might have done her or whether
she dripped the fatal liquid on his pudding or sloshed
it into his sherry. Grievances and disagreements:
can they lead the way to grace? If our thoughts
and feelings were soup or stew, would they taste
of bile when we're defeated and be flavored
faintly with grace on better days? I await the time
and place when you can tell me, little butter pear,
screeching monkey mind, wolf cub, curious furrow

browed mammal what you think of all this.
Till then, your bookish old aunt sends you this missive,
a fumbling word of encouragement, a cockeyed letter
of welcome to the hallowed ranks of the nerds,
nailed up nowhere, and never sent, this written *kiss*.

from *American Poetry Review*

Bust of a Young Boy in the Snow

◊ ◊ ◊

Odd place for a sculpture—
cemented to a newel post
on the front porch,
disarming the winter visitor
who wanted a good grip
and not this unsettling head
floating waist high.

Lips apart, ear like a split
oyster, rough erosion
crawling up his nape
and, over the cheek,
a verdigris birthmark.
Thankfully, his metal's

well beyond cold.
Souls may be stored
on planets, said Plato,
each of them mindfully
sowed in a star.
I think there's a live one
in every snowflake

falling for a shoulder,
the tip of a warm tongue,
better life in the new

world. They accumulate
on the child's brow,
his flat-topped hair,
tarnished dimple and fold

of neckskin. They bunch up
on his northeast side
like shivering immigrants.
The result is something to behold—
an elephant boy, a misshapen,
Phantom of the Opera mask
covering half his motionless face.
How often resurrection's

a slight miscalculation
of past, present, and future.
A cow nudging its dead
calf. A little boy's eyes
in winter,
opened rigid and wide.

from *Five Points*

The Death
of Winckelmann

◊　◊　◊

Trieste 1768

I

The Abbé Winckelmann was at his desk
in the hotel, when his new friend Francesco
returned, ostensibly in search of his
dropped handkerchief. He asked to see, once more,
the special medals from Her Holy Empress,
and Winckelmann obliged him merrily
by waving them like censers in the air.
Done with his "fair Antinous" charade,
Francesco made his move and pulled a knife,
intent on robbery. A fight ensued,
and Winckelmann was stabbed at least five times.
Some servant, hearing cries, surprised the thief,
who fled, with gory hands, into the street
and hid himself nearby inside a shed.
The Abbé staggered to the balcony,
pressing a cloth against his streaming wounds.

II

He'd argued that the turbulent Laocoön
embodied chaste decorum and restraint.
Sedateness was a virtue in itself,
for this bookish son of an epileptic cobbler.
Gripping the banister, he had become
a grisly simulacrum of the statue,
peering in desperation, faintly, down
into the dim and cavernous hotel.
A bustling group of servants mounted toward
him on the stairs, some shrieking in their panic,
until they reached him finally and hushed,
stopping to catch their breath before they tipped
him gently down onto a mattress. Then,
as though he truly were a wounded king
or holy martyr, some fell on their knees,
while some like saints or ancient Romans stood
and hid their pallid faces in their hands.

III

Poor Winckelmann had met his murderer
only the week before. Francesco heard
him asking about ships, and, butting in,
told Winckelmann that he knew of a captain
whose brigantine was ready to embark.
The two men set out for the quay but went
instead to a coffeehouse where both indulged
forbidden inclinations. They returned
to the hotel and were inseparable
thereafter, although both were unforthcoming.
The Abbé served as Papal Antiquary
and never told his friend. Francesco failed,
for his part, to disclose that he had just
been freed from jail. He thought the Abbé was
a spy or an adventurer, perhaps
a Lutheran or a Jew. At any rate,
there by himself, with money, in Trieste,

he made an easy mark for young Francesco.
The scholar had been frantic to persuade
his *amoroso* to return with him
and foolishly showed off a golden snuffbox,
a gift from the Marquis of Tavistock.

IV

He'd hoped to die held in the broken arms
of his beloved Apollo Belvedere
and glide through heaven pressed to that pure stone.
But now a guardsman thumbed his battered *Iliad*,
while a condoling monk assisted him
in drawing up a will, which he would die
trying to sign. Francesco, on the wheel,
would bawl and beg for death, then lie exposed
as fare for famished dogs and harbor fowl.
A courier, dispatched to Rome, would bring
the awful tidings to the Vatican.
Cassandra-like, Frau Kaufmann went to Mass,
and, trudging through the galleries, distraught,
Mengs wept before the Barberini Faun.
The medals were discovered by a cardinal,
uncatalogued, among the Abbé's things.

V

We have our own Apollo Belvedere,
which Winckelmann inspired, at the Met.
A grand Canova on the balcony,
of Perseus rampant with the baleful head.
The victor with his magic shoes and helmet
is otherwise stark naked in the court
of Polydectes, where he hoists his trophy,
high and dripping, up before the hall,
to petrify the whole licentious rout
and end the tyrant's terrible misrule.
The scene, at last, was what the gods had wished.

Our hero rode through town, pelted with flowers,
while pageants overspread the countryside.
Danaë rejoiced, the Nereids rejoiced,
Andromeda rejoiced in broken chains,
for Perseus had delivered up the palace
and greeted faithful Dictus with the crown.

from *The New Criterion*

My First Mermaid

◇　◇　◇

I

In Florida, where these things can happen,
we stopped at the last roadside attraction.

Into a small theater decorated with mold,
behind a curtain sagging like seaweed,

a wall of glass held back a wall of water.
And there in the springs, a woman in a bikini top

and Lycra fish-tail held an air hose to her lips
like a microphone. What was she waiting for?

Into the great open bowl of the springs,
a few fish drifted. They looked at the two of us.

They shook their heads and their bodies rippled.
Air bubbles shimmered in the filtered Florida sun,

each a silver *O* racing to the surface to break.
We'd missed the day an unscripted underwater blimp

of a manatee wobbled into view. The gray, whiskered lard
of a sea cow or the young woman who sang—

lip-synched, rather—some forgettable song,
her lipstick waterproof: which was the real mermaid?

II

Given the weight of water, nothing happens fast
to a mermaid, whether it's love or loss.

Not like the landlocked life, I wanted to warn her.
But here came a prince in street clothes,

trying to think thoughts that were heavy enough
to make himself sink to her level. His shirt ballooned,

a man made not into a merman but into a manatee.
Yet, in the small eternity it took for him

to grasp her greasy flipper, for her to find
his more awkward human ankle, and then

for them to turn, head over each other's heels—
a ring rolling away, too beautiful to catch—

they lived happily ever after.
Until one of them had to stop for breath.

from *The Kenyon Review*

EAMON GRENNAN

The Curve

◇   ◇   ◇

First thing to notice is the blunt integrity of the jet's engine,
snub-nosed and bursting with thrust-potential, perched
for takeoff under a cloudy sky, murmuring and growling
to itself in its own dialect of imperatives and unimpeachable
nouns, waiting the word to go. Then the series of radiant
explosions somewhere out of sight, the wild takeover into
the hands of chance, too fast for thought, and you keep going

into the blur of possibility becoming what is as is, and soon
—rising on this inhuman burst of speed—the world spreads
under you its miniature concerns: houseblocks and toy cars,
the snow-white tablecloths and handkerchiefs of fields,
the child's map of spider-roads studded with quill-trees,
the home ground shrinking to fit in the palm of your hand,
all creaturely concerns dimming and disappearing like
figures down the wrong end of a telescope. Then it is

cloudlife for a little while, the quick juddering of sudden
turbulence to put your heart crosswise, till you're above
that too and in the clear. And you could be alone up there
with a world of wonders under you, going on as if it were
all in your will and you intended it, and there's time
to see earth as simple landscape, something salvaged from
its own ungainly details by the saving grace of elevation,
the small unspoken hope it offers, till you're going down

again, descending, entering the cloud again and lost in it,
waiting, waiting, your heart all eyes winkling the mist
for a sign, the whole thing that holds you holding steady

in ways you can't begin to fathom, until this blind desire
of yours becomes a kind of Orpheus in the overworld,
a force of fixed attention bringing things to bear until
you're through, the green ground again rising to greet you.

from *Five Points*

DANIEL GUTSTEIN

Monsieur Pierre est mort

◇ ◇ ◇

My seventh-grade French teacher, Mademoiselle Torrosian, kept a pet rock, Pierre, who looked like an average potato. She made occasional mention of him, basking in his round holder on her desk, if it meant including him as an example for that day's lesson. *"Monsieur Pierre voudrait du bifteck et les pommes frites"* if we were learning to order a steak and fries. Or *"Monsieur Pierre aime juillet mais pas janvier"* if we were learning to distinguish between the months. Mademoiselle Torrosian dressed as a tablecloth, wearing a checkered yellow top above her dull brown pant legs. She had short hair and wide glasses, though I once caught her stepping out of Kramer Gifts, a shop at the mall where you could buy dirty decks of cards and fuzzy dice. A neighbor of mine, Kev Wilson, cooked up the plan to kidnap Monsieur Pierre, out of boredom, maybe, but it was easily accomplished: I slid the rock off its pedestal into my bookbag during the confusing crush at the end of class, and we had him. I'm not sure that Mademoiselle ever let on that Monsieur Pierre had gone missing, until we left her the first of our many ransom notes. Kev and I had cut the alphabet out of numerous magazines, the way we saw in the movies, and glued odd-shaped letters to construction paper, saying, in terrible French, *"Nous avons Monsieur Pierre"* for "We have Monsieur Pierre," and if she'd like him back unharmed, she'd give everyone in the class an "A." Mademoiselle Torrosian took to reading the notes out loud, correcting our French as she went, and then would utter pleas for his return. She would say, in earnest, *"Monsieur Pierre est mon bébé, mon petit oiseau bleu, ma chanson, et ma danse,"* or something like that, and the class would stare ahead without much sympathy. We, in turn, would write more and more perverse ransom notes, describing that we were cutting off Monsieur Pierre's ears, or putting out his *"oeil"* or breaking his nose. Mademoiselle Torrosian's brow would darken each time she entered the classroom and saw a new note lying on her chair. It was a small class; fifteen or twenty kids, and she probably guessed it was me and Kev, but then again, there was always that dickwad Marvin DeLeo, that girl, Angie, who always pronounced *besoin* as "boz-wan" and was always peeved when Mademoiselle corrected her, and Overman, too, that big, crazy, silent loon of a time bomb just waiting to throw someone out the window. Meantime, Monsieur Pierre resided in my backyard, in a regular area where many other rocks lived, and sometimes Kev and I would have a hard time distinguishing him from your typical shale, or quartzite, or whatever we were learning in earth science. One time, I put him in the oven, after my mother had begun baking a load of potatoes, and she freaked when she tried to stab him with her big fork, scratching him mightily. Kev and I used him as a hammer once, when we were trying to build a wooden ladder in the backyard, and there we chipped him, but the coup de grace came when we were tossing Monsieur Pierre back and forth in a game of "you're it" and he fell onto the patio and cracked in half, perfectly. We vowed to superglue him back together, a clear thin line of paste at the fissure, and soon afterward, I snuck him back into position, on his little round holder beside Mademoiselle Torrosian's grade book, even as Mademoiselle erased the blackboard. "Oh la la," she said, turning around a minute later. She held him up to the light, smiling, at first, then dropped him into the empty metal trashcan, where he landed with a good boom. *"Monsieur Pierre est mort*—dead," she said, then barked: *"Ecoutez!"*

from *Rhino*

R . S . G W Y N N

from *Sects from A to Z*

◇   ◇   ◇

High Anglicans (or *C. of E.*)
Are numerous far over the sea.
     They ring a small bell a lot,
     Read T. S. Eliot,
And burn incense in no small degree.

The Baptists put stock in immersion
And loudly will cast the aspersion
     That a ritual that stops
     With a few sprinkled drops
Is merely a watered-down version.

The blue-eyed Episcopal ladies
And gentlemen look like the Bradys.
     Their children are blond,
     And they all are quite fond
Of the Escalade and the Mercedes.

Fundamentalists think it's apparent
That the Bible is strictly inerrant.
     When one asks, once again,
     "Well, so *who* married Cain?"
They claim Yahweh was, singly, her parent.

A J.W. (Jehovah's Witness)
Should never be asked in to sit. Nes-

tle in, bolt your door,
Or you'll let in a bore
Who will point out your soul's lack of fitness.

The Mormons once had a hegemony
In Utah, allowing polygamy.
With their bearded heads hung
The men thanked Brigham Young,
Who responded, "Yes, wasn't that big of me?"

The Oneidans detected sin's essence
In all symptoms of manly tumescence,
So their men they unmanned,
Crying, "Take sin in hand!"—
A religiously planned obsolescence.

The Quakers possess inner lighting
And refrain from all feuding and fighting;
They enter their meetings
With "Bless thee" for greetings,
But the service is hardly exciting.

The Shakers thought sexual activity
Was a wastefully sinful proclivity:
"No more sleeping in pairs!
Go make tables and chairs!
Sublimate and increase productivity!"

Unitarians pray, but they never
Say to whom, and thus claim the endeavor,
While it's heavenward sent,
More precisely is meant
To address someone known as "Whoever."

The number of folks who use *X*'s
In spelling out *Christmas* perplexes.
It's truly inanity
(Just think *Xianity!*)—
A small matter, I know, but it vexes.

Most Zealots are eager to tell us
That their God is bad-tempered and jealous.
They go on for hours
Describing His powers
With a zeal that's excessively zealous.

from *Poetry*

Bird, Weasel, Fountain

◇　◇　◇

Seuss-like with its tufted yellow topknot
and roosting in a histrionic landscape—
snowcapped purple mountains, orange sunset—
the oddly crested bird in one of the paintings
upstairs in the Roerich Museum
stopped me on my last visit. Recognition
passed between us. I remembered it;
it seemed to have been awaiting my return.

Mounted by Balch of Lunenburg, the weasel,
wearing winter white, and with a mouse
eloquently dangling from its jaws,
takes my measure from its pedestal
low in a glass case in an exceptionally
dim corner of the Fairbanks Museum
and says quite plainly, though its mouth is full,
We'll know each other when you come again.

Solemn in their Pre-Raphaelite grace;
alert and sympathetic, though reserved;
ready to meet the gaze of anyone
who passes by, the figures in the fountain
at Riverside Drive and 116th Street
hold out their shallow goblets, mildly offer
the thirsty wayfarer a drink of water
and silently invite her to return.

The bird is not well painted, and the weasel
is badly lit. The fountain's low relief,

eroded by familiarity,
is hard to see—they all are—
without an effort. All three are too proud
and patient to call, *Here I am—remember?*
Given attention, I have things to say
to you, as you to me, if you return.

from *The Cincinnati Review*

Refusal to Notice Beautiful Women

◇   ◇   ◇

I don't know why I didn't think of this before.
It's so simple: I just won't notice.
Twenty years ago the hormones would have exploded this idea
but now I'm—now I have the wisdom of—anyway
I'll just be like "What? Oh, I didn't notice. Where?
Over there? Nope, didn't happen to see her."
Life is going to be a lot easier. I'll read more books;
I won't keep looking up when someone comes into the café
because who cares? I mean,

to hell with them! They want to be so impossible?
They want to be so many versions of sublimity on two legs?
Let them go watch each other, whatever, let them go tantalize
lurching iron pumpers who wear backwards baseball caps.
Or let them go get engagement rings from suits that wear cologne,
vice presidents with tickets to Jamaica. I'm very vague on all that
because I'm so devoted to other values. Like,
art's endless campaign to represent the mysteries of the spirit's
passage through the realm of time and change. That's
what I'm all about—but I get distracted I mean till now I did
get distracted by BWs but that's over. Finito.
Let them shimmer and slink in Jamaica,
let their bikinis be murderous—
that's only flesh! Flesh is nothing but—you know, it's only meat.
It's only physical substance. With whatever warmth and smoothness
ultimately it's—well, the seventeenth-century guys called it dust
and they had a point. Were they happy? Well,

that's not my problem. I've got very large bookstores I can go to
where a thousand books are shiny and smooth—

I abjure Jamaica. I extract Jamaica from my heart
with the tweezers of mature sobriety. Not that I had any actual access
okay okay anyway I have this life now: I embrace it.
My jeans are wearing through at the knees. I embrace this.
My hair, to the extent that it remains, points northeast in a peculiar way
since my last haircut by Dawnette who is much less sexy than her name
and who calls to mind a vat of mashed potato—but I don't say that
because she's human, plus I'm not thinking about how any woman looks.
Yesterday I spilled ginger ale all over the seat of my gray Mazda—
all right. It's my life. I accept it. The thought that a BW is unlikely
to ride in an old gray Mazda coated with ginger ale does not come up.
I read books. Oh,
perhaps on occasion I recall that in 1967 Kathy Farley smiled at *me*
on Thayer Street but I know that has become fiction, she is fictive,
and I'm off now to a very large bookstore,
and once I've got a tall mocha and some slim volumes in the café
even the Michelle Pfeiffer of 1983 couldn't make me look up.

from *Michigan Quarterly Review*

JIM HARRISON

On the Way to the Doctor's

◊ ◊ ◊

On Thursday morning at seven a.m. seven surgeons will spend seven hours taking me apart and putting me back together the same way. Three of the surgeons don't have medical degrees but are part-time amateurs trying to learn the ropes. One is a butcher who wants to move up. A butcher's salary is twenty-seven thousand and the average surgeon makes two hundred twenty-seven, the difference being the proximity of the nearest huge asteroid to the moon, which could be destroyed any minute now. In anticipation of the unmentionable I've put my life in order. Anyone with blood-slippery hands can drop a heart on the floor. I've sent a single-page letter of resignation to the *Literary World* but they haven't had time to read it. They're exhausted from reading Sontag's obituaries, a nasty reminder that everyone dies. Assuming I survive, Jean Peters and Jean Simmons will re-emerge as twenty-seven-year-olds and trade shifts nursing me around the clock. They're goddesses and never get tired. Since the surgeons are cutting me open like a baked potato, sex will be put aside for the time being. It's unpleasant to burst your stitches on a Sunday morning dalliance when you're due on your gurney in the hospital Chapel of Black Roses. I'm not afraid of death. I've been told I'll immediately return as a common house finch but it's all the stuff between here and death falsely called life. Right now we're actually in the car with my wife driving to the doctor's. I say, "Turn left on Ruthrauff onto La Cholla." I always drive when we go to Tucson but I'm in too much pain half-reclining in the seat peeking out like the little old man I might not get to be. At the entrance to the office the doctor meets us with an immense bouquet of Brazilian tropical flowers. The doctor resembles a photo of my mother in 1933, so much so that I'm uncomfortable. The office is full of dozens of identical framed photos of a desperate sunset in the desert trying to look original. The office temperature is kept at 32 degrees to reduce odors. I've been recently sleeping under seven blankets and am quite cold. The pages of the magazines on the coffee table are blank so that you can make up your own *National Geographics*. I haven't eaten for days except rice and yogurt but my wife is out in the car having a baguette stuffed with prosciutto, imported provolone, mortadella, and roasted peppers. They turn out the lights so my eyes don't tire reading blank pages. Now I see that the mirror on the wall is two-way and in another room the seven surgeons are rolling up their sleeves, hot to get started. "We don't have time to wash our hands," they say in unison.

from *New Letters*

ROBERT HASS

The Problem
of Describing Color

◊   ◊   ◊

If I said—remembering, in summer,
The cardinal's sudden smudge of red
In the bare gray winter woods—

If I said, red ribbon on the cocked straw hat
Of the girl with pooched-out lips
Dangling the wiry, black-nosed lapdog
In the painting by Renoir—

If I said fire, if I said blood welling from a cut—

Or flecks of poppy in the tar-grass-scented summer air
On a wind-struck hillside outside Fano—

If I said, her one red earring dangles from her silky lobe,

If she tells fortunes with a deck of fallen leaves
Until it comes out right—

Rouged nipple, mouth—

(how could you not love a woman
who cheats at Tarot?)

Red, I said. Sudden, red.

from *The New Yorker*

Hour

◇　◇　◇

My sixth sensurround
is down, my second skin
the skin I'm stepping
into: I lick
a new finger & hold it up
to the wind: O my beloved
what. O
my beloved what. O my
beloved shovel-nosed mole
can I clean the soil
from your black, sightless eyes
can I massage with fine oils
your tiny, webbed feet
are you tired of running
into drainpipes
does your mouth foam
approaching power lines
are your tunnels collapsing
do you have work to do
does the dirt breathe
do you breathe the air
between the dirt
are your lungs
the size of earlobes
do you hear me
in the tunnel next to you
have you cut your nose
on a shard of glass
have you excavated

the severed, blue leg
of Spider-Man
did you pause to admire
his red booties
are you tunnels collapsing
do you have work to do
am I keeping you
am I keeping you

from *CROWD*

Talk

◇   ◇   ◇

like a nigger is what my white friend, M,
asked me, the two of us alone and shirtless
in the locker room, the bones beneath my skin

jutting like the prow of a small boat at sea,
the bones beneath his emitting a heat
that turned his chest red and if you're thinking

my knuckles knocked a few times
against his jaw or my fingers knotted
at his throat, you're wrong because I pretended

I didn't hear him, and when he didn't ask it again,
we slipped into our middle-school uniforms
since it was November, the beginning

of basketball season, and jogged out
onto the court to play together
in that vision all Americans wish for

their children, and the point is we slipped
into our uniform harmony, and spit out Go *Team!*,
our hands stacked on and beneath the hands

of our teammates and that was as close
as I have come to passing for one
of the members of The Dream, my white friend

thinking I was so far from that word
that he could say it to me, which I guess
he could since I didn't let him taste the salt

and iron in the blood, I didn't teach him
what it's like to squint through a black eye,
and if I had I wonder if he would have grown

up to be the kind of white man who believes
all blacks are thugs or if he would have learned
to bite his tongue or let his belly be filled

by shame, but more important, would I be
the kind of black man who believes silence
is worth more than talk or that it can be

a kind of grace, though I'm not sure
that's the kind of black man I've become,
and in any case, M, wherever you are,

I'd just like to say I heard it, but let it go
because I was afraid to lose our friendship
or afraid we'd lose the game—which we did anyway.

from *Gulf Coast*

BOB HICOK

My career as a director

◇   ◇   ◇

It's the last moment of night in the theater.
The names of the best boy and key grip
are floating toward heaven. The movie
was about the paralyzing sadness of death
and the last movie I saw in this theater
with my feet up on the balcony
was about the paralyzing sadness of death
but the name Albert Albertson is funny.

His job was to shout, *Quiet on the set*
when the actors were about to be sad
or die. And the director's job was to ask
if the actors could be sadder, if they could die
better. And the makeup crew
drank together in parking lots and hotel rooms,
always looking at the sky or the bedspreads
for the true colors of sadness, the spooky hues
of death. If the last two movies I've seen

had babies together, I'd pay to meet
their offspring in this theater from the 1940s,
recently restored and staffed by volunteers
who enjoy Portuguese films about the struggle
to eat good food and Norwegian films
about the agonizingly beautiful noses
of Norwegians. The firstborn
would be an overachiever of sadness,
the dead people would die again
so they could be mourned again by the long shot

of birds swirling at sunset like scatter
is what becomes of us. The secondborn

would be shy and have water in every scene
and at least one actor would smile
and a bicycle would lean against the wall
of the cottage, where after three bottles
of wine, the four couples who've come
from the city for a week of the dishes
being magically done after their feasts
and the beds being magically made
after their partner-swapping sex, discuss
the paralyzing sadness of death while a fire
suggests that the cycle of life is beautiful
though not energy efficient. In the third,

a man would read a letter twenty years
after it was written by his mother
about the day they played in the sandbox.
She described how sunlight was trapped
in his hair and that he leaned back
and kissed her shin and how after they buried
his green soldiers to their heads,
they pulled them out and set them free
on the sea of the birdbath. She wrote
the letter just after they played,
while looking out the window at another woman
tying the shoe of a little girl, we would see her

at her desk in a flashback after everyone
who would die in the movie has died,
after everyone who would scream has screamed,
after the cup that would look glorious
and symbolic has looked gloriously symbolic,
has glowed on the counter like it can never fade,
though behind and around it everything does.
When he folds the letter and puts it back

in the envelope and comes down from the attic
and touches the hair of a woman who is sleeping

on the couch and carrying how close we come
to being eternal in her womb, the movie will end
with the opening of her eyes, eyes that were cast
because they are brown like the richest soil
and I will sit in the dark while the names
ascend, the sadness of the movie feeling false
because there's so much of it until the lights
come on and people feed their arms to the appetite
of their coats and faces flow back into skin
and minds return to bodies and bodies recall
how brief they are and I will live in my creaking
seat until the screen catches fire again.

from *The Gettysburg Review* and *Poetry Daily*

KATIA KAPOVICH

The Ferry

◇　◇　◇

I'm jotting down these lines,
having borrowed a pen from a waitress
in this roadside restaurant. Three rusty pines
prod up the sky in the windows.
My soup gets cold, which implies

I'll eat it cold. Soon I too
will leave a tip on the table, merge
into the beehive of travelers
and board one of the ferries,
where there's always a line to the loo
and no one knows where the captain is.

Slightly seasick, I keep on writing
of the wind rose and lobster traps,
seagulls, if any—and there always are.
Check the air and you'll see them
above straw hats and caps.
The sun at noon glides like a monstrous star-

fish through clouds. Others drink iced tea,
training binoculars on a tugboat.
When I finish this letter, I'll take a gulp
from the flask you gave me for the road
in days when I was too young to care about
those on the pier who waved goodbye.

I miss them now: cousins in linen dresses,
my mother, you, boys in light summer shirts.

Life is too long. The compass needle dances.
Everything passes by. The ferry passes
by ragged yellow shores.

from *Harvard Review*

At Gettysburg

◊   ◊   ◊

The one I love stands at the edge
of a wheatfield, wearing
a blue cap, holding
a plastic musket in his hands. The one I love does a goofy

dance at Devil's Den. Mans a cannon. Waves
at me from a hill. He

dips his foot into Bloody Run. The sepia
dream of his dead body
is pulled by the water
over the rocks. And I

am the shadow of a stranger taking
his picture, laid
out like so much black
drapery on the pavement. Is there

some better explanation? Was there

some other mossy, meandering
path we might have taken

to this place through time and space? Why

is it that where my heart
should be, there's a small
bright horse instead? While I

was simply standing
over there by a stone, waiting, did an old
woman run her bony
hand through my hair, and leave
this gray ribbon there? The one

I love leans up against a fence, and then
pretends to be shot. He

opens his eyes
wide and grabs his chest, stumbles
backward, falls
gracefully into the grass, where he lies
for a long time holding the sun in his arms. I take

another picture there. The worms

beneath him make
the burden of the earth light enough to bear—and still

inside me I believe I carry
the pond where the injured
swans have come to flock. I
believe I hold inside me
the lake into which the beautiful armless mortals wish to wade. I am

their executioner and their creator, after all, being
as I am, their mother. Were

they gods who came to earth to die and suffer, I wonder, or

boys who died and turned into gods? O,

the one I love needs sunblock, I think, too late,
and, perhaps,
a bottle of water, but now
I have no idea where we are. *Where*

were you, God asks, *when I
spread out the heavens and the earth? If you*

were not there, then how
can you expect to know where you are now? Truly,

I don't know. I look around.
I say, *We're lost,*
to the one I love, who

looks over my shoulder and laughs.
No, Mom, he says and points to dot and arrow
of ourselves
on the map.

You're holding the battlefield upside down.

from *New England Review*

Just a second ago

◇   ◇   ◇

I had an urge to toss my drink across the visiting poet's shirt.
　　　Hello. I liked your reading.
Red wine spreading into the whiteness
　　　It was a wonderful reading
of his shirt. My hand—my glass—
is still full.
　　　Yes. People starting to drift to the cheese and bread.
At the wedding, the organist stops,
the minister smiles benignantly. She thinks of touching the bride's breast.
　　　Hello. I liked your wedding.
It's amazing: Traffic stays on its side of the road.
What keeps it there, really? I trust
no one will stand up and scream when I am a bride.
I don't laugh when I hear someone has died.
You're sitting there quietly right now

very
very quiet.

The slightest noise could cause an avalanche.

It's scary when someone gets pushed onto
　　　Hello. I liked your reading
the subway tracks.
So scary when someone walks into Wendy's
and shoots the people eating.
　　　　　　　　What I almost did
just a second ago

while you were crossing the street
while you were finishing your lunch
while you were handing me your terrible secret. . . .

from *The Cincinnati Review*

Seventeen Ways from Tuesday

◊   ◊   ◊

At the Miró exhibit in the Centre Pompidou,
           I hear a guy say to his girlfriend, "When we get back to the hotel,
                     I'm going to put it to you seventeen ways from Tuesday,"
and I think, now what does that mean, exactly?
           I know what "it" is, but why that number and that day?
           Also, what is it about art that makes people so happy?
It's probably seventeen because that's a funny number,

as the comedians will tell you: one through six aren't,
           seven through twelve are, thirteen through fifteen
                     are duds, and anything from seventeen on is funny again.
And when you're trying to get sexy with somebody,
           it's probably a good idea to suggest, not slapstick
           or parody or satire and certainly not farce, travesty,
caricature, burlesque, *opera buffa*, buffoonery, miming,

squibbing, lampooning, or Hudibrastics—
           especially not Hudibrastics—but, instead, good humor,
                     or, better, a good nature, i.e., a tender one.
As for the day, that's easy: you rest on Sunday, you take care of
                     the first part of the week's work on Monday
           so you can start thinking about your fun from Tuesday forward,
and now there are only four days left for that,

but you being you, you won't offer that special someone
           you share all your fun with a mere four choices
                     but the square of four plus one.
Now about art: art makes people happy because—
                     well, let's see what Miró has to say on the subject.

This is from a 1936 interview with Georges Duthuit
in *Cahiers d'Art*: "Painting and poetry are done

in the same way you make love; it's an exchange
of blood, a total embrace—without caution,
without any thought of protecting yourself."
Hmm. You're right, reader: that does sound pretty stupid!
Ha, ha! Tell you what, Joan:
you hang on to your day job there! To put it another way,
you leave the inkpots alone, and I won't start

splattering the canvases! I think art makes people happy
because it makes them feel like children again,
spoiled children: even though we're tiny and penniless
and half their size, the grown-ups are doing everything they can
to please us—look, here's a roomful of paintings,
a two-and-a-half-hour movie, a book as thick as a mid-size city's
telephone directory, and there's more on the way!

Later I see the young lovers in the museum cafeteria,
and they seem broodish, distant from one another.
I wonder if he has followed up on his original
playful proposition with something less playful
and more manlike, i.e., doggy. If so, then
he should make short work of his *blanquette de veau*
avec sauce béchamel and maybe reach over and finish off

the *coq au Riesling* she has barely touched and coax her
into returning with him to the exhibit, for Miró at his best,
that is, when painting, not writing, is childlike,
fastening wire or feathers to paper and connecting them
into busy little villages with a single freehand line
or daubing in great balloons of color that threaten
to burst from the frame or concocting entire universes

of bugs and dunce caps and yin-yang symbols
and leering pollywogs and big nameless buttocky doodads
that seem to be part of a strange dream, yeah,
but a fun dream, not a disturbing one,
and even when he is painting figuratively

71

(yes, he did that, too), he produces, not
a conventional portrait *à la* Degas or even the young Picasso,

but one of a thick-haired guy in weird Catalonian peejays
       leaning up against a Japanese print,
           the whole set against a background of yellow
as bright as egg yolk or gold or the sun itself.
             Lovers, be like painters, i.e., playful, not grim.
      Painters, you be like painters, too! Leave the writing to us.
And you know what to do already, poets, so get busy.

from *Subtropics*

The Laws of Probability
in Levittown

◇   ◇   ◇

I've been smoking so much pot lately,
I figure out what my poems are going to do
before I write them, which means when I finally
sit down in front of the typewriter . . . well . . . you know . . .

I moved back in with my parents,
and I'm getting really good at watching TV.
Soon as I saw the housewife last night on *Inevitable Justice*,
I knew her husband was the killer and I told her so and I was right.

Remember whenever Jamie Lee Curtis would come on
TV and we'd yell, *Hermaphrodite!* all happy? I maintain
her father, Tony, is an American treasure, and have prepared a mental
list of examples why, so should we happen to meet again, my shit's backed up.

There were too many
therapists in the city—97% of all therapists
are certifiable ding-dongs by nature, which is fine
if you live in Platteville, Nebraska, where there's only

like three therapists in the entire town
(the odds are in your favor), but if ten thousand
therapists are lurching around the streets, chances are
one thousand will be 100% batshit nuts.

I had a choice between watching

Robert Frost talking about his backyard
on *Large American Voices* and Farrah Fawcett on *True Hollyweird.*
I chose Farrah, because I knew what was going to happen, and I was right.

Here's something I've been trying
to work in: *10 rations = 1 decoration.*
What do you think? *10 monologues = 5 dialogues,*
10 millipedes = 1 centipede, .000001 fish = 1 microfiche . . .

I've got a million of those.
I wrote them down, back when I was
writing things down. But I've been thinking I should
tip the Domino's kid more than a buck on 14. Should I?

from *The Hat*

Found

◇   ◇   ◇

My wife waits for a caterpillar
to crawl onto her palm so she
can carry it out of the street
and into the green subdivision
of a tree.

Yesterday she coaxed a spider
into a juicier corner. The day
before she hazed a snail
in a half-circle so he wouldn't
have to crawl all the way
around the world and be 2,000
years late for dinner.

I want her to hurry up and pay
attention to me or go where I
want to go until I remember
the night she found me wet
and limping, felt for a collar
and tags, then put me in
the truck where it was warm.

Without her, I wouldn't
be standing here in these
snazzy alligator shoes.

from *Iodine Poetry Journal*

Sally's Hair

◇　◇　◇

It's like living in a lightbulb, with the leaves
Like filaments and the sky a shell of thin, transparent glass
Enclosing the late heaven of a summer day, a canopy
Of incandescent blue above the dappled sunlight golden on the grass.

I took the train back from Poughkeepsie to New York
And in the Port Authority, there at the Suburban Transit window,
She asked, "Is this the bus to Princeton?"—which it was.
"Do you know Geoffrey Love?" I said I did. She had the blondest hair,

Which fell across her shoulders, and a dress of almost phosphorescent blue.
She liked Ayn Rand. We went down to the Village for a drink,
Where I contrived to miss the last bus to New Jersey, and at 3 a.m. we
Walked around and found a cheap hotel I hadn't enough money for

And fooled around on its dilapidated couch. An early morning bus
(She'd come to see her brother), dinner plans and missed connections
And a message on his door about the Jersey Shore. Next day
A summer dormitory room, my roommates gone: "Are you," she asked,

"A hedonist?" I guessed so. Then she had to catch her plane.
Sally—Sally Roche. She called that night from Florida,
And then I never heard from her again. I wonder where she is now,
Who she is now. That was thirty-seven years ago

And I'm too old to be surprised again. The days are open,
Life conceals no depths, no mysteries, the sky is everywhere,

The leaves are all ablaze with light, the blond light
Of a summer afternoon that made me think again of Sally's hair.

from *The Kenyon Review*

MARK KRAUSHAAR

Tonight

◇ ◇ ◇

Whatever it is about this poor schmuck
crashing his beater Plymouth into a light pole
then scaling a chain-link fence in socks and no shirt,
cheek bleeding, Mets cap backward
I'm not sure, but suddenly
he's running through somebody's yard
and half vaulting, half falling over a trash can,
he trips into the street,
where he's hit by a bus.

He scrambles up and five cops cuff him
and yank him and drag him to the flashing
black-and-white where they take care—careful—
he doesn't bump his head getting in.
So on this mid-autumn Saturday night
it seems to be God's way
to let this sad man stick up an all-night store
and show the whole bleak story
on the TV in front of which

in order not to think about Louise
I imagine those strange cells that move along
the bloodstream looking to colonize and multiply.
And I can see the planning and packing too,
and I picture them waving to friends and setting sail.
Adenoma, she's told me.
And I'd bet she was no more than leaning over
to pick up a key when the first cell got restless,
tying her scarf or rinsing a pear or

buying a brush when the first cell ship
steamed slowly north to a spot in her lung.
If there's something to learn here I don't know
but I think of the rich cells chatting with
the handsome captain and I imagine the poor cells
slurping soup in steerage, but even now
as the young man with the scraggly beard
and torn pants grins into the camera
I imagine it must be God's way

to arrange that I lie on the green couch with white trim,
God's way to arrange a magazine opened to page
eighteen, a dime by the door, a pen on the chair,
the neighbor's dog's now continual barking
through which I hear the last of the traffic:
a car and now another car,
a couple of semis double clutching, one
with cargo of ballpoints maybe, a second
with a trailer of wing nuts and canvas shoes.

from *The Gettysburg Review*

JULIE LARIOS

Double Abecedarian:
Please Give Me

◊   ◊   ◊

Anything & anybody but Freud, that Bic-and-Pez-
Bitten, cylinder-obsessed, Big-Cigar-as-Envy
Calamity of a man who posited the idea that sex
Dachshund-style with Mom might possibly show
Evidence of a troubled mind. How did every concave *V*
Female its way into his convex psyche? *Mon dieu,*
Gott im himmel, por el amor de dios—just one night
How I'd like to translate myself without the shrinks.
I wouldn't get lost in fog, I wouldn't be a beggar
Jumping off the Pont Neuf, wouldn't be a twisted *Q*
Knocking up some *U* with my tail, nor a Lap-
Lander hitching myself to my own sled. No,
More likely I'd just be sitting looking for a reason
Not to stop sitting. There'd either be me in this dream,
Or some smoke and some midgets. Does all hell
Position itself for a couched session with that sick
Quill-and-quiver-addled Viennese? He's still the Raj
Royale of our subsurfaces, isn't he, the Rabbi
Sigmund ben Oedipus? He makes even bowls of mush
Turn into latent tendencies, while we keep cranking
Up his sirens without any downtime or relief.
Virility as a red fire hydrant, lust as a long flagpole?
Where on this earth, or where off it, do these bad
X-rated verticalities escape from his narrative arc?

Yes, the shapes of this world go from arrow to orb,
Zero is a pierced hole. But what a lot of hoopla.

from *The Georgia Review*

Demographic

◊　◊　◊

It's time for me to walk to the bus stop
and sit down among them, the man
tied into his wheelchair, the woman
with the humped back, time for me
to kneel and hold his cup while he adjusts
his books and his pack, look up at her
flowered blouse, his scratched glasses.
There's a sky full of rain that won't
come down, pigeons asleep on the lawn,
and across the street pumpkins piled high
in front of the market, Xeroxed flyers
stapled to the telephone pole. To the east
a day moon above the bridge, cars
filing under like a school of fish,
and if I look down at my feet I won't
knock over the plastic dish the blind man
has filled to the brim for his dog. It's time
to go to work, to wait while they gather
their belongings, while the metal mesh
platform unhinges and bangs down,
time to nod to the driver as he pulls
back on the lever and a man lifts
into the air, to cup her elbow, a thin wing
sharpened by suffering, to enter
the threshold and stand among them,
listen to their murmurs, the news

of the day, to slip my hand through
the frayed canvas noose and hold on.

from *Alaska Quarterly Review*

That's Not Butter

◇   ◇   ◇

Once upon a time there was a house full of divorced women who did not sew
No beautiful little red coats or beautiful little blue trousers.
The children's clothes, purchased at Sears,
mass produced, not very unique, but good enough.

Every month the fathers would visit and take the children to fun places,
like the amusement parks, Chuck E. Cheese, and church bazaars.
No beautiful green umbrellas or lovely little purple shoes
with crimson soles and crimson linings.
Only flammable stuffed monkeys and glow sticks.

Most of the time, the children were on their own and passed
time shoplifting glue and smoking skinny cigars in the woods.
One day Little Pink Brittany found a jungle and suggested they explore.
"That jungle smells funny," warned Little Peach Paulie.
"Not as funny as your mom," laughed Little Taupe Tabitha.
"Let's investigate, maybe ganja grows wild there."
Little Mauve Melvin's eyes twisted left. "We could cultivate
the ganja, become gangsta farmers, start our own syndicate!"

The children proceeded, they proceeded to get lost in the jungle.
The jungle owls were warming up, one by one the children cried.
By and by they met a tiger. "Aren't you all adorable in your
matching little yellow sweats and little yellow hoodies.
I could eat every single one of you right up!"
"Who are you?" asked Little Amber Ambrosia.
"Why, I'm the grandest tiger in the jungle!"
Up above in the treetops the leopards laughed. "Not in those stripes!"
The tiger shook his paw in the air. "Haters!"

"It's almost night, you kids shouldn't be here. It's not safe.
Climb on my back and I'll take you home to your mothers."
"We're not leaving without the ganja!" protested Little Beige Timmy.
The tiger sighed, "There's no ganja in this jungle, only coconuts."

But the children knew this was a lie for they could smell the ganja,
the tiger smelled as if he had been soaking in it from birth.
Little Auburn Emily pulled out her sharpened toothbrush and demanded,
"The ganja or your hide! You're not the boss of me!"
That tiger somehow seemed to know how to think like a tiger,
like a paranoid tiger stoned out of his whiskers. Instead of gobbling up
the little children, he ran, round and round a tree,
faster and faster until he was whirling round so fast his legs
could not be seen, it was more that just a blur, he was melting,
melting away until there was nothing left
except a great pool of melted butter.

"Can we smoke that?" inquired Little Speckled Sarah.
"I don't think so, but I bet we could cook with it," said Little Freckled Furman.
So the children scooped up the butter in their sneakers
and found their way home after torturing a turtle for directions.

When the mothers saw the melted butter, they were pleased!
"Now we'll all have pancakes for supper!" and the whole family
sat around a huge big plate of most lovely
pancakes, yellow and brown as little tigers. The mothers each ate
twenty-seven pancakes, the fathers came over and each ate fifty-five,
and the children each ate a hundred and sixty-nine
because they were so hungry.

from *MiPoesias*

Eyes Scooped Out
and Replaced by Hot Coals

◇ ◇ ◇

The above, the punishment, the mild
but just punishment, symbolic,
the great advancement our planet
most needs.
The procedure is painless,
using methods currently available
only in cartoons. Polls were taken,
it was voted upon overwhelmingly in favor.
The justness of it,
known in the bone
by each of our nation—is undeniable. Thus, it is proclaimed,
on this day anno domino, etc., I, the final arbiter
and ultimate enforcer
of such things (appointed by the king!), make official
and binding, this: that the eyes shall be gouged out
and replaced by hot coals
in the head, *the blockhead*,
of each countryman or woman who,
upon reaching their majority,
has yet to read
Moby Dick, by Mr. Herman Melville (1819–1891), American novelist
and poet.

from *Five Points*

PAUL MULDOON

Blenheim

◇   ◇   ◇

Small birds were sounding the alert
as I followed her unladen
steed through a dell so dark and dank
she might have sported the waders
her grandfather had worn at the nadir
of his career, scouring the Outer Banks
for mummichog and menhaden.
Those weeks and months in the doldrums
coming back as he ran his thumb
along an old venetian blind
in the hope that something might come to mind,
that he might yet animadvert
the maiden name of that Iron Maiden
on which he was drawing a blank.

from *Five Points*

Albert Hinckley

◊   ◊   ◊

Miss Crandall's Boarding School for Young Ladies of Color,
Canterbury, Connecticut, 1833

Last Sunday, a white boy openly smiled at me
where I sat with my sisters at the back of the Baptist church.
When the pastor spoke of the sin of slavery,
the white boy looked back with his eyebrows arched.
I could read his thoughts, but I dared not meet his glance,
for nothing must pass between us, not one chance
for gossip to pounce with glee on one shared smile.
No one must think of us as eligible girls.

Waylaid by ruffians as we reached the ford,
our wagon was overturned. Our sodden skirts
weighted and slowed us, but no one was hurt.
Splashing to me, his eyes looking truly scared,
that boy took my hand. *"Let me help you, miss.
From this day forward, I am an abolitionist."*

from *The Cincinnati Review*

RICHARD NEWMAN

Briefcase of Sorrow

◇   ◇   ◇

"Some writers get into the habit of letting of name a metaphor without really showing the image to the reader: sea of life, mattress of the soul, river of death . . . or (perhaps the worst) briefcase of sorrow."
—Frances Mayes, The Discovery of Poetry

My briefcase of sorrow slumps by the door.
The semester's done. I leave it behind,
all my manila folders of grief (stacked
and alphabetized, bound with rubber bands
of stretched hope), pens of overachievement,
and pencils of petty angst. At some point,
I suppose I should dump its insides out
on the table, the staple remover
of apocalypse, a few sticky notes
of indecision. Poor briefcase—it can't
ingest them, try as it may, and I should
especially purge the gradebook of mixed
endeavors, the crumbs of last month's sandwich.
Not now. My neighborhood pub calls louder
than some cloying briefcase, strap of pity
wagging as I leave, its two bright buckles
of expectation gleaming for my return
once again, when I will spill its contents,
the paperclips of despair, the Wetnaps
of desire, bringing it, light and swinging,
along my side to fill one more time its
compartment of everything and nothing.

from *Crab Orchard Review*

The Poet with His Face in His Hands

◇   ◇   ◇

You want to cry aloud for your
mistakes. But to tell the truth the world
doesn't need any more of that sound.

So if you're going to do it and can't
stop yourself, if your pretty mouth can't
hold it in, at least go by yourself across

the forty fields and the forty dark inclines
of rocks and water to the place where
the falls are flinging out their white sheets

like crazy, and there is a cave behind all that
jubilation and water fun and you can
stand there, under it, and roar all you

want and nothing will be disturbed; you can
drip with despair all afternoon and still,
on a green branch, its wings just lightly touched

by the passing foil of the water, the thrush,
puffing out its spotted breast, will sing
of the perfect, stone-hard beauty of everything.

from *The New Yorker*

DANIELLE PAFUNDA

Small Town Rocker

◊   ◊   ◊

We took up for each other where our families left off. Left a mess
of crumbs and beer cans. A pile of laundry. When you left town,
I kept your T-shirt in bed, synthetic residual warmth.

Used to be I'd meet you at the train tracks. My shirt too close
to my skin, my hair cramped with sexy. Used to be at night,
and red lights would come rolling across. The water below
was cut with a hacksaw.

First night in a new city, and you said it wasn't sex. She had her back
to you. When I said *I don't care,* I was in the parking lot
with my fist on my forehead. With bare feet and a bus ticket.
No ledge. No lock me in the trunk; you'd sooner lock me in the engine.

So much later you found a phone booth. Called me up
on my new red phone. I felt like the Commissioner, or like Batman
on the wrong end of things. I heard the thrum-thrum of your voice,
your lighter click, the little signs. I took off my target T-shirt, I took off
my shiny pants. I stripped down quietly and I unplugged my lights.

from *The Canary*

The Sharper the Berry

◇　　◇　　◇

Nose out of joint, City Slicker?
Blown a gasket, Hot Shot?
Fit to be tied, Arty Farty?
Going through the roof, Curtain Raiser?

Sometimes you get the bear, sometimes the bear gets you.

Can't put the toothpaste back in the tube, Clever Dick?
Chewing nails and spitting tacks, Front Runner?
Got your knickers in a knot, your panties in a wad, Sexy Thing?

Every rose has its thorn.

Popped a vein, Man-of-the-World?
Rubbed the wrong way, Lean-and-Mean?

Worse things happen at sea.

Worked into a lather, Bold-as-Brass?
Blood at a boil, Dressed-to-the-Nines?

It's not the end of the world.

Tomorrow is another day, All-Wind-and-Piss.
It's always darkest before the dawn, Bottom-of-the-Heap.
There is a light at the end of the tunnel, Thick-as-a-Brick.
Behind the clouds, the sun is shining, Back-to-the-Wall.
After the rain comes a rainbow, All-Work-and-No-Play.
Midnight is where the day begins, Beats-His-Meat.

Chin up! With visions of redemption,
walk against the crowd, Down-at-the-Heels.

If you can't enjoy your own company, how can anyone else,
Drama-Queen?

Everyone might hate you, but at least you're still alive,
Button-Pusher.

from *New American Writing*

Race

◇　◇　◇

Huey Tran and JPEG Nguyen were the two best street racers in Frogtown
Even though they shared one car
Cuz goddammit that shit was expensive
JPEG's family was almost middle class
Huey's wasn't
so although it was really JPEG's Celica
Huey was the better racer and the better mechanic
And he could make that car sing on the road
boy
Sing so loud that they called it Linda Trang Dai.

So Huey and JPEG were like a team
JPEG's real name was Nimoy cuz his parents
Came to America and watched Star Trek and
They thought Nimoy was an American name
Now Nimoy called himself JPEG because he thought he was

SO
　　　　PRETTAY

But Huey called him Nimoy which bugged him but hey
what are you gonna do.

So one Saturday night they heard the whiteboy wanted to race them.
Whiteboy's real name was Todd Landers but everyone called him
Whiteboy or Poseur or Fuckhead cuz though he spent hella money
souping up his Ford Focus most of that shit was cosmetic—
Like the spoiler which he carefully painted to match the paint job on his car,

A gigantic fin sticking up from the back
Like a whale's tail stapled to a guppie.

Some called Whiteboy the Mandarin because he had
Kanji tattoos on his arms that he thought said
Strength in love but really said something like
Unreliable delivery service
And he would wear a purple satin coat with dragon and phoenixes
Which made him look like Confucius threw up all over him
While drunk.

Anyway he wanted to race Huey and JPEG for pink slips
Which was fucking stupid cuz they didn't want his car anyway
And no one really races for their cars
Unless they have a Hollywood contract
But Whiteboy wanted to race and he said if he won
He would get some free tune-ups from Huey and if Huey won. . . .

Well, what?

Huey thought about it and said if I win, you give me that
Wack ass purple satin jacket you wear all the time
And Whiteboy laughed and said that was fine so
Huey called his girl Vina who borrowed the car earlier
To take her dad to INS for some bullshit paperwork
and Huey and JPEG didn't need the
Car that day anyway since they both had the day off
From the garage, business had been slow since
Most "real Americans" wanted their "real American cars"
To be fixed up by "real Americans"—
So they were just gonna hang out and play Gran Turismo all day.
Vina drove over to Huey's place with the yellow Celica
screeching the tires as she pulled up to the curb
Which made JPEG say goddamn I think sometimes
She drives that car faster than you.

And they all hopped in and drove over to Snelling and Ford Parkway
And Vina remembered to take her pink Hello Kitty pencil case
From the glove compartment that held her .22

See her mom got her the gun when she went off to college
Cuz she heard those crazy white frat boys be raping women all the time.
She figured if her daughter wanted to go so far away for college
She should have some protection, so Vina's mom, tough country girl
From Thai Binh, went next door to the café where all the Viet hoodlums
Drank coffee and played cards
And asked one of them to buy her a gun for her baby girl.
So Vina took out the little dividers inside the pink plastic Hello Kitty pencil case
And put the .22 in there (perfect fit!) and had been carrying it around
Since college cuz some habits are hard to break.

JPEG told her to take the gat out of the glove compartment
Cuz it would weigh the car down and Huey just laughed
At his dumb ass and asked Vina how the car was running
Fine she said so they rolled up and saw that a small group
Of people had come through to see the race.

And they saw that the white dude was wearing his purple mandarin coat
And he said there's nothing on under this cuz it's a race and I'm gonna win
And Vina said if you let that whiteboy win I'm never gonna speak to you again
And JPEG said why don't you just shoot him in his foot, Vina,
And Huey got out of the car and said hey what up, Jarvis,
And the whiteboy said my name's not Jarvis

And the crew that had gathered was mostly Asians
Though it had enough different colors to be a Benetton ad
And Vina said they should all hold hands and sing "We Are the World"

But it was decided that Huey would race against Fuckhead
So about half the crowd stayed at the starting line and half drove
Down to where the finish would be and so Huey got behind the
Wheel of the Celica and Whiteboy got into his Focus with the
Big fakey-looking spoiler and the Kanji stickers that he thought
Said *Fast and Furious* but really said
Szechuan Chicken
And with a wave from Vina they were off

Into

FIRST GEAR
And Huey was feeling pretty good cuz
Fuckhead Mandarin Whiteboy was already kinda behind
And Huey knew that he was gonna mess up shifting into

SECOND GEAR
And everything is getting faster now and Huey starts getting excited
Because although at first he thought beating this fool in this race was
Going to be more like punching the clock he was starting to feel it a little
Bit especially as he shifted into

THIRD GEAR
And the engine purrs like a cat who just had speed pills
mixed into its Meow Mix and the hum starts thrumming from
the wheels to the top of his head and the wind starts making
waves around the windshield of the Celica and he starts
worrying about whether the cops will show up or not and he
starts laughing a little bit and he shifts into

FOURTH GEAR
and Huey swears to God that the spoiler is like a sail as he
slithers down the sleek roads wet with neon perspiration and
the streetlights are whizzing by so fast that they look like
they're Ping-Pong balls popping past the table of the horizon
and he gets a little scared now scared enough to laugh a little
more and that whiteboy wannabe wankster waste is so far
behind he can't even dream of catching up

FIFTH GEAR
and his head is spinning like a desktop globe and his eyes are
like the finger that'll stop it looking for home and every pock
on the tar is caressed like pores on a lover's face by this car
that he spends hours on in its maze of tubes and wires trying
to learn its secret language trying to get it to laugh and go
just a tad faster and now its only direction is forward like
some type of dancer snapped from a slingshot and the night
sky is doing that Star Wars Millennium Falcon thing and he
wonders if JPEG will let him call him Chewbacca which
makes him laugh even harder and the other cars and the city

lights and the dandelions that stick up like sunflowers from
the boulevard streak past air blowing against the Celica like
a warning breath, life flashing in front of the headlights like
kids in Saigon on a Sunday on their mopeds all cool glares
and upturned chins and cigarette ash and SARS-looking
mouthmasks

and it's all over. And a few split seconds later Whiteboy
Fuckhead Jarvis Mandarin's car crosses the finish line
and he's getting out of his car asking if they're really gonna take
his jacket.

And Huey says hand it over.

Motherfucker, JPEG adds.

And the three of them,
Young, beautiful, and Vietnamese,
Walked back toward their car, not knowing where they were going
But knowing they would get there together
And as they were about to get into the Celica
Vina turned to their pale defeated opponent
And said
In case you haven't noticed,
This was all a
Race
Thing
And you lost.

from *Michigan Quarterly Review*

DONALD PLATT

Two Poets Meet

◇   ◇   ◇

for Carlos Drummond de Andrade and Elizabeth Bishop

When my two favorite poets in the whole infinitely worded world met,
            and they met
only once, it was by chance on the sidewalk at night in Rio,

            and they had just come out
of the same restaurant, where they had eaten at separate tables. Drummond
            had had the humble

tutu, black beans mixed with manioc meal, and fried bananas. Elizabeth the
            gringa had wolfed down
a caper and pimento picadinho served with farofa, manioc farina larded

            with butter, sausage,
and eggs. Both had drunk cachaça with chasers of beer. The acacias
            were in full bloom

and lit the street with their yellow globes. Their faint scent
            could not conceal
the smell of urine from the side alley where the drunks would piss

            copiously and with great
long-winded sighs. The panhandlers were out with their chorus of coughs
            and por favors.

Lota, who knew everybody, introduced them. Elizabeth had not yet
                    started to translate
Drummond's verse. Drummond had never read any of Elizabeth's

                    few poems, which shone
like a single strand of pearls against a black funeral dress. Because they were bo
                    "supposed to be very shy,"

they said little and spoke only the formalities
                    in Portuguese,
which was Elizabeth's third, half-learned language.

                    But when Lota
had taken Drummond's arm and whispered that there was someone
                    he must meet,

he was anything but gauche. He bent over Elizabeth's
                    outstretched
hand and put his lips, which had once murmured, "Love in the dark,

                    no, love
in the daylight, is always sad," briefly to the dry skin
                    of the back of her hand.

Let it be recorded that in the life where people meet and pass
                    there was a kiss
in the middle of a sidewalk. In the middle of the sidewalk, this kiss.

                    from *The Iowa Review*

The Great Poem

◇   ◇   ◇

The great poem is always possible.
Think of Keats and his odes.
But you shouldn't have to be dying.

What I'm writing now is not
the great poem. After a few lines
I could tell. It may not even be

a particularly good poem, although
it's too early to decide about that.
Keep going, I say. See what happens.

But trying hard is one of the problems,
since it shows in the lines as a strain
or struggle that reminds the reader

too much of the writer, whereas
most readers want to listen alone.
The great poem, I think, will arrive

when I no longer care. Perhaps
I'll have abandoned art altogether,
and I won't even want to write

the poem down. But then I'll remember
what I once would have given
for this moment, and I'll go back

to my desk. And I'll write the poem
as though I were another person,
someone I will never be again.

from *Nightsun*

Roadside Special

◊   ◊   ◊

Finally
I got my own roadside special.
A new car!
The color of this ink, Laser Blue, Mazda PR5 '03
No more
'88 Honda Accord, no power steering, jinxed transmission
No more
'86 Jeep Cherokee 4wheel drive, turned on a dime
No more
'70 red Opal GT, complete with Fred Flinstone rust below the feet
No more
'72 white VW camper, my son gets that hippie van pop-up
No more
Chevy wagon you like so much
No more
Plymouth rust colored short lived won't run special
No more
Toyota Corolla, ooh la la runs forever, but sold it
No more
Volvo engine block cracked, sold on the side of the road, aqua blue
No more
$500 special Mercedes sedan with no brakes. What year?
No more
White egg Geo Metro that was kissed by a rose of an elderly woman's foot who
missed the brake, Odna's red Cadillac, lucky the kids weren't playing in the street
No more
'70 yellow Beetle that froze up in the driveway
No more

'86 Sentra wagon that we bought new but didn't change the oil
and seized up by the Mobil station
No more
'68 army green Dodge Dart that $75 wonder from Delaware that
carted dead chickens in the trunk and housed the farm dog in the
front chewed up bench seat that we replaced with Trans Am bucket
seats and rammed an old dresser in the backyard with, demolishing
it into splintered pieces
No more
'72 Oldsmobile station wagon we called "The Growler" that got time and chain
troubles on the GWB in NYC full of Electrolux vacuum cleaners that some
stocking-hooded van-riding men thought they'd steal as we bolted up the hill by
the side of the road to the nearest gas station.

I say no more to old toys and cars.
Those sentimental male pieces of
"Gotta have it, such a deal!"
Send back the '76 Catamaran
and the '72 Glastron orange pop motorboat.
Old adolescent memories wanting to make sure
you're still alive with your youthful vigor.
An old canoe will do for me—but new.
Quiet and simple, uncomplicated.
Men want complicated toys and simple relationships.
Women want simple toys and "interesting" relationships.
I won't say complicated because they are anyway, why say it?
No more roadside specials.
Those beckoning boats and cars
that litter the rural roadways like lawn furniture.
"Come buy me!" it says
"Come look at me!"
The unsuspecting gullible male like a homing pigeon
devoted to crashing says,
"Look at that! Will you look at that!"
The car you're riding in pulls over
and the next thing you know
a strange man is negotiating
over yet another roadside special!
Can't we just get blueberries?

Or a fresh tomato?
Why does it have to be this
unusual '70 black El Camino?

from *Endicott Review*

The Other Woman's Point of View

◇   ◇   ◇

I've never loved anyone more than I love you, he said,
which meant what, exactly? Perhaps he'd never loved
anyone less, either. He could not help
lying—to make people feel better.
Yet he made everyone feel worse
with his young-old-man's grimness, and sagging mouth.
He laughed inanely,
wore ties he liked to call "dangerous,"
endangering his thin neck.

He'd say, You make me so very happy,
with such mournful and tear-stained
eyes, she prayed she never would see him sad.
After making love he'd sob, then pretend
he'd only lost his breath. Be safe, won't you?
I won't, she said, I'll run with scissors in my hands,
I'll go outside with a wet head. He never got the jokes.
She too was melancholy.
He seemed to think they should nail up public notices of guilt.
He didn't want to disappoint his mother, or his friends
or his first girlfriend, who was the only woman
who had agreed to marry him. He'd begged her
to love him, so she had left her old life
of misery behind, and began a brand-new one with him,
which they perfected over time. She'd bought him
a lovely onyx and silver ring

which he wore even when he was furious
—which is to say
he never took it off
even when galloping over her.

from *The Kenyon Review*

Discounting Lynn

◇　◇　◇

I find it in the twenty-five-cent bin,
which I browse biweekly for the book
that will explain why my hand
seems so misty lately, even
with my new glasses on,
why it can't hold on to anything
with the grip of commitment,
not even a fork, which looks
unsettling these days,
like half a set of silver teeth,
so I bend down low and I choose.

This book has been through a lot.
Since it's poetry, I imagine
it had trouble finding a publisher,
so now rub in this further indignity:
abandoned by the bookseller
at a discount of 25%, and then
dumped by the first owner for profit
in a used bookstore ($9.70—
how pathetic, not even $9.99)
relegated then to an even more desperately
used bookstore ($2—handwritten
on a round orange sticker)
and now given up for lost, now
25¢ slashed sloppily in pencil on the flyleaf.
The book looks fairly readable, a Lynn
wrote it. Maybe not, though, maybe just
a pseudonym. Actual name possibly

Lila-Jean, someone trying to abridge
her native floridity, sound more seriously
friendly, solid, actual, northern.

I find the right spot to read this book:
under an oak tree whose acorns are so small
they seem toylike underfoot, scattered by a child's
imagination, not capable of reproduction
or supplying half a squirrel's midnight snack,
here beside the Muffler 'n Brake Shop
and two dumpsters. Stacked railroad ties
form a half-bench beneath the tree.
A place where you can smoke a cigarette
and in effect throw yourself away
to prepare for reading this thrice-junked text.
On the backleaf some notes are scribbled
by one of the owners, presumably the first,
who invested the most to read the book
and needed a return on that investment.

many characters are doing something on the page

I don't mind the lack of punctuation, but I do
like a thought and I think
how fortunate I rescued this book
from such a dodo:

book draws you out of the text

and really it says *texl* because she was so
done with this book she couldn't bother
to cross her *t.* Well, honey, good riddance.
I can't help thinking she. Does some post-
Paleolithic, prefeminist corner of my psyche
suspect that men still tend not to buy
slender poetry paperbacks by Lynns?
But at least there's some substance
to that note and I read some pages to see
if there's anything in it. Could be.
What if this Lynn were to become our era's

Dickinson? What if she already is!
Then I start writing this because my hand
feels misty again, "Lynn" hasn't helped
one jot. Nor has anti-Lynn, or whoever
said the words Lynn's ex-reader wrote,
since it could have been a professor
with a name like a sneeze. Dr. Hatchitt.
I write this on the backleaf, weaving in
and out of his/her scribbles. Then I relent
because an author can't be blamed for her
readers and turn to the last page of texl,
where authors tend to plant their most
magic beans, and just as I'm getting
to the sentence that is about me, I'm
stung on the back of the hand by a sweat bee.
But the sentence turns out to be about Lynn,
Lila-Jean, not me. And I'm not sweating at all,
or I wasn't then, and officially that was no bee.

from *Failbetter*

KAY RYAN

Thin

◇　◇　◇

How anything
is known
is so thin—
a skin of ice
over a pond
only birds might
confidently walk
upon. A bird's
worth of weight
or one bird-weight
of Wordsworth.

from *Poetry*

A Phone Call
to the Future

◇   ◇   ◇

1

Who says science fiction
is only set in the future?
After a while, the story that looks least
believable is the past.
The console television with three channels.
Black and white picture. Manual controls:
the dial clicks when you turn it, like the oven.
You have to get up and walk somewhere to change things.
You have to leave the house to mail a letter.

Waiting for letters. The phone rings: you're not there.
You'll never know. The phone rings, and you are,
there's only one, you have to stand or sit
plugged into it, a cord
confines you to the room where everyone
is also having dinner.
Hang up the phone. The family's having dinner.

Waiting for dinner. You bake things in the oven.
Or Mother does. That's how it always is.
She sets the temperature: it takes an hour.

The patience of the past.
The typewriter forgives its own mistakes.

You type on top sheet, carbon, onionskin.
The third is yours, a record of typeovers,
clotted and homemade-looking, like the seams
on dresses cut out on the dining table.
The sewing machine. The wanting to look nice.
Girls who made their dresses for the dance.

2

This was the Fifties: as far back as I go.
Some of it lasted decades.
That's why I remember it so clearly.

Also because, as I lie in a motel room
sometime in 2004, scrolling
through seventy-seven channels on my back
(there ought to be more—this is a cheap motel room),
I can revisit evidence, hear it ringing.
My life is movies, and tells itself in phones.

The rotary phone, so dangerously languid
and loud when the invalid must dial the police.
The killer coming up the stairs can hear it.
The detective ducks into a handy phone booth
to call his sidekick. Now at least there's touch tone.
But wait, the killer's waiting in the booth
to try to strangle him with the handy cord.
The cordless phone, first noted in the crook
of the neck of the secretary
as she pulls life-saving files.
Files come in drawers, not in the computer.
Then funny computers, big and slow as ovens.
Now the reporter's running with a cell phone
larger than his head,
if you count the antenna.

They're Martians, all of these people,
perhaps the strangest being the most recent.

I bought that phone. I thought it was so modern.
Phones shrinking year by year, as stealthily
as children growing.

3

It's the end of the world.
Or people are managing, after the conflagration.
After the epidemic. The global thaw.
Everyone's stunned. Nobody combs his hair.
Or it's a century later, and although
New York is gone, and love, and everyone
is a robot or a clone, or some combination,

you have to admire the technology of the future.
When you want to call somebody, you just think it.
Your dreams are filmed. Without a camera.
You can scroll through the actual things that happened,
and nobody disagrees. No memory.
No point of view. None of it necessary.

Past the time when the standard thing to say
is that, no matter what, the human endures.
That whatever humans make of themselves
is therefore human.
Past the transitional time
when humanity as we know it was there to say that.
Past the time we meant well but were wrong.
It's less than that, not any more a concept.
Past the time when mourning was a concept.

Of course, such a projection,
however much I believe it, is sentimental—
belief being sentimental.
The thought of a woman born
in the fictional Fifties.

That's what I mean. We were Martians. Nothing's stranger
than our patience, our humanity, inhumanity.

Our worrying about robots. Earplug cell phones
that make us seem to be walking about like loonies
talking to ourselves. Perhaps we are.

All of it was so quaint. And I was there.
Poetry was there; we tried to write it.

from *The Georgia Review*

VIJAY SESHADRI

Memoir

◇　◇　◇

Orwell says somewhere that no one ever writes the real story of their life.
The real story of a life is the story of its humiliations.
If I wrote that story now—
radioactive to the end of time—
people, I swear, your eyes would fall out, you couldn't peel
the gloves fast enough
from your hands scorched by the firestorms of that shame.
Your poor hands. Your poor eyes
to see me weeping in my room
or boring the tall blonde to death.
Once I accused the innocent.
Once I bowed and prayed to the guilty.
I still wince at what I once said to the devastated widow.
And one October afternoon, under a locust tree
whose blackened pods were falling and making
illuminating patterns on the pathway,
I was seized by joy,
and someone saw me there,
and that was the worst of all,
lacerating and unforgettable.

from *The New Yorker*

Misjudged Fly Ball

◇　◇　◇

Just before he died,
when Tim had come back
from his dream of dying
to tell us it was all
just bush league, Little League,
why the hell did I waste
time fearing it? I thought

of that moment when the ball's
hit and you start in and,
uh-oh, should have gone
the other way and all
you can do is watch it arc
over your clumsy scramble
to reverse direction—

too late too late, why
hurry, and anyway
isn't the lifelong
fought-against sensation
of defeat now nearly
irresistible, a sweetly
growing spaciousness

in which the celebration
at home plate shrinks
to nothing, and the cut-
off man, no longer shouting,

or waving, turns away
to kick his glove in tiny
dust clouds down the infield?

from *The Cincinnati Review*

CHARLES SIMIC

House of Cards

◊   ◊   ◊

I miss you winter evenings
With your dim lights.
The shut lips of my mother
And our held breaths
As we sat at a dining room table.

Her long, thin fingers
Stacking the cards,
Then waiting for them to fall.
The sound of boots in the street
Making us still for a moment.

There's no more to tell.
The door is locked,
And in one red-tinted window,
A single tree in the yard,
Leafless and misshapen.

from *Virginia Quarterly Review*

Homesick

◊   ◊   ◊

I was reading again and French apples
were on my mind and oranges the way they sold them
in giant carts and how the skin was thick and
loosened from the flesh and how it made an
orange saucer where you placed the sections
after you pulled the threads away, the ugly word
pith, it's called, and raspberries with cream—
and how it would have been if I had stayed
in the same hotel another eight or ten years and
married someone else—it always comes to
that—and taken up another trade,
for as you know what we call nostalgia
is for the life we *didn't* live, so much for
homesickness, and I am homesick too for
southern Spain, where I didn't live, but mostly for
Mogador (where I didn't live) with the tiny
white streets and blue shutters, one store the
flutes on one side, the drums on the other, the synagogue
smaller than the African Methodist church
on North Governor Street in Iowa City
before they rounded us up, though we had two days,
for we had spies, to tear the linings open
and sew our jewels in and our thousand-franc notes,
although we had to leave our heavy furniture
behind, and Libby's picture, when we boarded
the plane for Paris, more like the camel that took us
to live with the Berbers in the Atlas mountains
twenty-five hundred years ago than not like,
all of whose fault it was that Ezra who preached

the ups and downs; and how the Berbers welcomed us,
and how the French put us in crowded rooms
and made us sit for hours, for they believed in
égalité, so everyone should die of
boredom equally and *Vive la France* and
Hail to the Eagle and Rah, Miss Liberty,
one of her breasts exposed—I have nostalgia
for your life too, what are you, Mongolian?
Don't leave the rugs behind, milk the horses!
Are you a Russian? You are great at this.
Light the samovar! I give you my past for
nothing. Here is your number. Line up, my lovers!

from *Ecotone*

The Loser

◇   ◇   ◇

The pressure was on, and I don't perform well under pressure. "You're the champ," Jenny said. "You always succeed. Come on, Travis, you can do it." I stared out the window at the rain. "I'm a loser. I've always been a loser. Even when I've won, it's felt like losing. When I was three years old, I was convinced I would never get anything right. I don't blame anybody. It's just a feeling that permeates my very soul," I said. "But you can do anything, Travis. I've seen you. You're amazing," Jenny said. "That's just fooling with people. Sure, I can take a car apart and put it back together again, but what does that prove? I can build a house to keep you out of the rain, but I'm not fooling myself. That's another matter altogether," I said. "You're too hard on yourself," Jenny said. "And what about all those mountains you've climbed? Everyone says you're the best. And all that money you've made through good, honest, hard work?" "That's kids' stuff. Believe me, I'm a loser. I never get anything right," I said.
We'd had this conversation a hundred times before. It annoyed me to no end, not the stuff that Jenny was saying. She meant well, and I knew it. But my part. It sounded so ridiculous. "Why are we even talking about me?" I said. "You started it," she said. "I asked you to kiss me, and you sort of fell apart." "That's funny, I don't remember that at all. I thought you asked me if I was going to compete in the tennis championship," I said. "I don't know anything about a tennis championship," Jenny said. "I was just feeling a little warm and cuddly, and wanted a kiss." "I'd be more than happy to kiss you," I said. "No, no, the mood's passed. I'm more worried about your soul,

why you feel that you will never get anything right," she said.
"Did I say that? I've always found that when people start
talking about their souls it's best to leave the room," I said.
"Do you want me to leave the room?" Jenny said. "No. Of course
not. I'm not talking about my soul, am I? Or am I?" I said.
"You were earlier, just for a second. I could leave and
come back. Or I could leave and not come back. Whichever
you prefer. It's your soul. Perhaps you'd like to be alone with
it," she said. "I feel like I'm caught in a whirlpool. I'm
dizzy and I'm sinking. Isn't there anything we can talk about
other than my soul? After all, it's just a butterfly, it's just
a poof," I said. Jenny walked into the kitchen and started
banging some pots and pans around. I shook my head and stood up.
Something was terribly wrong. An egg was hatching in my hand,
the egg of an otter. Otters don't lay eggs, but I was starving.

from *Crazyhorse*

Body English

◇　◇　◇

I'd seen a golfer's body curve
into a deep parenthesis as the ball
inched toward the cup, and I knew
how mothers in the bleachers leaned
and flapped their useless wings
when their child's kick arced perfectly
before descending shy of the goal.
As the two men from the funeral home
maneuvered my mother's body
through the narrow, sloping hallways
of her eighteenth-century cape
to where the black van had reversed its way
up the steep slope to the porch,
I cowered with my father and my sister
in a distant bedroom, waiting
for their footsteps and the thumps
against the woodwork to abate.
Through a narrow opening in the door
that centuries of weather had warped
so that the latch no longer fit
we glimpsed the stretcher as they carried it
across the porch. *Alley-oop!* one said
as the other raised my mother's bare feet
high, letting her head, so newly sprouted
with winter wheat, tilt dangerously
downward. Suddenly the three of us
were on our feet—bodies craned,
chins lifted skyward—as if by pitching

all our weight we could prevent
the next bad thing from happening.

from *The Connecticut Review*

TONY TOWLE

Misprision

◇   ◇   ◇

someone said Sappho could be understood
only through her original tongue
and I said I didn't think so
as educational as that would probably be

someone wrote that Charles VIII
entered France in the 1490s
and I said to myself: I don't think so
he was born many years before that
but he did penetrate Italy in 1494
as far as Naples, and didn't withdraw
for an entire year, which seems extraordinary
by today's standards
but he finally lost virility and everything else
by hitting his head on a doorway in 1498

someone wrote that gardening was a literature
in which scholars nibbled at the edges
of what appeared to be an insurmountable edifice
and I thought that makes perfect sense
nibbling is an authentic scholarly pursuit
and eventually the edifice will get lower
and can be surmounted

somebody said that cretins painted murals
and got out of labyrinths but that seems unlikely
and someone wrote to say it's time for a poetry museum
but I don't understand how anyone could possibly know that
and isn't that what our books are already

glassless vitrines
where you're allowed to run your fingers over the art
or nibble on the implications
or loiter in the white passageways between the lines
hoping to meet the lenders to the exhibition

from *LIT*

ALISON TOWNSEND

What I Never Told You About the Abortion

◊   ◊   ◊

That it hurt, despite the anesthetic,
which they administered with a long needle, shot straight into the womb.

That they hit the vagus nerve the first time and I fell down when I tried to stand.
That after the second shot my legs snapped shut—

instinctively as any wild mother protecting chick, kit, cub.
That I held the hand of a young Hispanic nurse and wept

when she said, "You know, hon, you don't have to do this."
That I believed I did, though I nearly got up and left.

That the doctor was crude, saying (when he saw me conscious),
"It's always the ones who want to be awake who should be put out."

That dilation and curettage is exactly what it sounds like:
opening, scraping, digging out a scrap of tissue that clings.

That mothers both create and take life. That I crossed a picket line
to get into the clinic. That I wanted to come back another day

but knew if I left then I wouldn't return. That my mind was not,
as I let you believe, made up that night at Planned Parenthood,

the positive lab slip shining in my hand like a ticket to heaven.
That this was where the deep root of sadness began to take hold.

That I stood in our bedroom a few days before the "procedure,"
my blouse open and bra undone, looking at my breasts, marveling

at the way they swelled, even at eight weeks, like fruit I'd never seen,
remembering the rise and fall of my mother's body as she nursed my sister.

That I felt *inhabited* then. Incarnate, the cells of my skin glowing,
bright and scared. That I wished we were married, though it seemed uncool.

That I wished you'd said, "A baby? Let's do it!"
instead of "It's your body. You decide."

That it was all surgical and neat, not even
any blood afterward on the Kotex that made me feel fourteen.

That I dreamed of it for weeks. That we married years later, that dream
torn between us. That I had wanted to feel the hard bowl of my belly.

That I believed it was practical—you in grad school,
no health insurance, me the one with a job.

That the table I lay on was cold. That there was a poster
of a kitten dangling from a tree limb, with the words "Hang in there, baby"

on the ceiling above me. That I turned names
over and over in my head like bright stones:

Caitlin, Phoebe, Rebecca, Siobhan.
That the nurse wept with me, like some twentieth-century

Southern Californian fate, midwife to death
in her uniform printed with flowers.

That she wrapped my hands in her navy blue sweater.
That I described the thumb-size embryo inside me in all the obvious ways—

shrimp, peanut, little bud-wanting-to-open.
But not baby, never baby.

That I saved the paperwork as proof I'd been admitted
to the college of mothers. That I told you a good story,

letting you believe I believed I might not be able to write with a child,
that *this* was the beginning of the end of us.

That though we are kind now, and always cordial when we meet,
a decade after our divorce, it is the one thing I cannot forgive you.

That it has taken me twenty years to find words for this story.
That no matter how many *that*s I write, there are not—will never be—enough

from *Margie*

Counterman

◊   ◊   ◊

—What'll it be?

Roast beef on rye, with tomato and mayo.

—Whaddaya want on it?

A swipe of mayo.
Pepper but no salt.

—You got it. Roast beef on rye.
You want lettuce on that?

No. Just tomato and mayo.

—Tomato and mayo. You got it.
. . . Salt and pepper?

No salt, just a little pepper.

—You got it. No salt.
You want tomato.

Yes. Tomato. No lettuce.

—No lettuce. You got it.
. . . No salt, right?

Right. No salt.

—You got it.—Pickle?

No, no pickle. Just tomato and mayo.
And pepper.

—Pepper.

Yes, a little pepper.

—Right. A little pepper.
No pickle.

Right. No pickle.

—You got it.
Next!

Roast beef on whole wheat, please,
With lettuce, mayonnaise, and a center slice
Of beefsteak tomato.
The lettuce splayed, if you will,
In a Beaux Arts derivative of classical acanthus,
And the roast beef, thinly sliced, folded
In a multifoil arrangement
That eschews Bragdonian pretensions
Or any idea of divine geometric projection
For that matter, but simply provides
A setting for the tomato
To form a medallion with a dab
Of mayonnaise as a fleuron.
And—as eclectic as this may sound—
If the mayonnaise can also be applied
Along the crust in a Vitruvian scroll
And as a festoon below the medallion,
That would be swell.

—You mean like in the Cathedral St. Pierre in Geneva?

Yes, but the swag more like the one below the rosette
At the Royal Palace in Amsterdam.

—You got it.
Next!

from *Shiny*

Harvesting the Cows

◇　◇　◇

Stringy, skittery, thistle-burred, rib-etched,
　　　they're like a pack of wolves lacking a sheep
　　　　　　but also lacking the speed, the teeth, the wits—

they're heifers culled from the herd, not worth the cost
　　　of feeding and breeding and milking, let loose on a hill
　　　　　　one-third rock, one-third blackberry bramble.

And now, the scrub stung black by hard frost,
　　　here come the young farmer and his father,
　　　　　　one earnest, one wizened, wind-whipped, sun-whipped,

who make at the gate, from strewn boards and boughs,
　　　a pen, and park at its near end the compact
　　　　　　silver trailer, designed for two horses—

it waits at the mouth of the rutted tractor-trail
　　　descending through trees, an artificial gulley.
　　　　　　Up goes Junior, hooting, driving them down.

So much bigger than wolves, these sixteen cows:
　　　head to flank or flank to scrawny flank,
　　　　　　they can't turn around; but what they know is *no*:

some splash over the walls of the small corral,
　　　one, wall-eyed, giddy, smashes away
　　　　　　the warped plank that's propped on the far side,

crashing across alders and wet windfall
in a plausible though explosive dance, which prompts
another to aim herself at the same hole,

too late: the plank's back up, she's turned to the clump
and soon swimming among them, their white necks
extended like the necks of hissing geese,

but so much bigger than geese. When the younger man
wraps one neck in his arms, the cow rears up
and he goes down, plaid wool in shit-slicked mud;

so then the elder takes her by the nose—
I mean, he puts two fingers and a thumb
inside the nostrils, pulls her into the trailer.

The rest shy and bunch away from the gate;
a tail lifts for a stream of piss; one beast
mounts another—panic that looks erotic—

and the herdsmen try guile, a pail of grain
kept low, which keeps the head of the lead cow low
as though resigned, ready for the gallows.

The silver loaf opens, swallows them in,
two by two by two, and takes them away.
Hams need to be smoked, turkeys to be dressed out

here in Arcadia, where a fine cold spit
needles the air, and the birch and beech let go
at last their last tattered golden rags.

from *The Kenyon Review*

The Driver

◇   ◇   ◇

It's a safe car. It belongs to somebody else,
        And you've parked it legally near the right doorway,
                And you've made sure there's a tank of gas
And the engine's running okay. You're going to sit here
        As if you were supposed to sit here, which
                You are, minding your own business. You expect
Others to do likewise. Your driver's license
        At first glance looks pretty much like you,
                And when the others, dressed like customers,
Come out of the bank, they'll climb in by themselves
        And handle everything they're carrying
                By themselves, and as soon as all their shoes
Are off the pavement, you'll go. You've got the route
        All picked out. You know where to turn,
                Where to go fast, where you have to slow down
And drive like a tourist. But now the fat old lady
        In a twenty-year-old Lincoln is backing in
                Ahead of you, lurching, half-clutching,
Half-braking a foot at a time, and stalling it
        Two feet from the curb, and a hotel limo
                Is double-parking, almost touching you street-side,
Unloading baggage, and a kid in an orange Edsel
        Is jamming in back of you, half in a bus zone,
                And bailing out on an errand, and a cop
Is resting his pale-blue elbow on the roof
        Of the passenger side and looking in at you
                As the others scramble out of the door behind him,
And the cop says, smiling and nodding, "You guys kill me,"
        And strolls away while they take their time deciding

Whose turn it is to sit in the jump seat,
Who gets the outside window, who gets to choose
The first station, and the lady in the Lincoln
Steps on the wrong pedal and goes zooming
A half a block. The limo glides after her.
A City Transit tow truck has its hook
Under the Edsel and is hauling it off,
And as you drive away under the limit
The tall buildings on each side of the street
Grow even taller, and ticker tape and confetti
Come spilling down around you. Crowds on the curbs
Are cheering as loud as sirens. You raise the roof
So the guys in back can stand up and enjoy it
Out in the open, right in the sunshine,
Waving and grinning, taking green handfuls
Out of their satchels and tossing them up for grabs.

from *Margie*

Prayer to Tear
the Sperm-Dam Down

◊   ◊   ◊

Because we need to remember / that memory will end, let the
womb remain / untouched.
—from "Prayer to Seal Up the Wombdoor" by Suzanne Paola

Because we know our lives will end,
Let the vagina host a huge party, and let the penis come.

Let it come nude, without a raincoat.
Let it come rich, and leave with coffers drained.

Throw the prostate's floodgates open.
Let sperm crowd the womb full as a World Cup stadium.

Let them flip and wriggle like a mackerel shoal.
Let babies leap into being like atoms after the Big Bang.

Let's celebrate fullness, roundness, gravidity.
Let's worship generation—this one,

And the next, and next, forever.
Let's adore the progression: protozoan to guppy

To salamander to slow loris to Shakespeare.
Forget Caligula. Forget Hitler. Mistakes

Were made. Let's celebrate our own faces
Grinning back at us across ten thousand years.

Let's get this straight: Earth doesn't care if it's overrun—
if it's green or brown or black, rain forest, desert, or ice pack.

A paper mill is sweet as lavender to Earth,
Which has no sense of smell, and doesn't care

If roads gouge it, or industries fume into its air.
Beetles don't care. Or crows,

Or whales, despite their singing and big brains.
Sure, rabbits feel. Spicebush swallowtails

Feel their proboscides slide into flowers'
Honeypots, which may feel too,

But lack the brains to care. Even if beagles
Are as mournful as they look—

Even if great apes grieve, wage war, catch termites
With twigs, and say in sign language,

"Ca-ca on your head," they still don't care.
Or if they do—well, join the club.

We humans care so much, some of us dub life
A *vale of tears*, and see heaven as oblivion.

Some pray, for Earth's sake, not to be reborn.
Wake up! Earth will be charred by the exploding sun,

Blasted to dust, reduced to quarks, and still not care.
If some people enjoy their lives too much

To share, let them not share. If some despise themselves
Too much to reproduce, let them disappear.

If some perceive themselves as a disease, let them
Take the cure, and go extinct. It's immaterial to Earth.

Let people realize this, or not. Earth doesn't care.
I do, and celebrate my own fecundity.

I celebrate my wife's ovaries, her fallopian tubes
Down which, like monthly paychecks,

Gold eggs roll. I celebrate the body's changing.
(Might as well; it changes anyway.)

I celebrate gestation, water breaking,
The dash to the hospital, the staff descending,

Malpractice policies in hand. I celebrate
Dilation of the cervix, doctors in green scrubs,

And even (since I won't get one) the episiotomy.
I'll celebrate my bloody, dripping son, head deformed

By thrusting against the world's door.
Let it open wide for him. Let others make room for him.

Let his imagination shine like God's.
Let his caring change the face of everything.

from *Atlanta Review*

Ponies

◇   ◇   ◇

When the ponies are let out at dusk, they pound into their pasture,
pitching and bucking like the brutes their genes must dream they still
are.

In their shaggy, winter-coarse coats, they seem stubbier than ever,
more diminutive, toylike, but then they begin their aggression rituals,

ears flattened, stained brown teeth bared, hindquarters humped,
and they're savage again, cruel, all but carnivorous if they could be.

Their shoes have been pulled off for the season, their halters are rope,
so they move without sound, as though on tiptoe, through the rising
mist.

They drift apart now, halfheartedly nosing the stiff, sapless remnants
of field hay; sometimes one will lift and gaze back toward the barn.

A tiny stallion lies down, rolling onto his back first, then all the way flat.
A snort, rich, explosive, an answering sigh: silence again, shadows, dark.

from *The Atlantic Monthly*

Sex Elegy

◇ ◇ ◇

My lovers have vanished. I used to have many.
One moved to Boston and married a Japanese photographer.
Another became a famous actress. Another one, who for a long time
I mistakenly believed to be dead, now lives in Manhattan.

We used to know each other so intimately,
sucking and munching on each other, inserting,
penetrating, exploding. Becoming as one. Funky
smell of sweaty bodies. Clothes strewn on floor
and bed. Candles burning. Smoke of cigarettes and joints
curling up the bedroom atmosphere. Now we never touch,
barely talk. Some I have lost all contact with.

But memories of our pleasure together, my dears,
still play in my mind. My body can still feel your touch.
My tongue still remembers your taste.
Everything else I seem to have forgotten.
The present is the life insurance premium automatically
deducted from your paycheck, while the past burns
out of control in a vacant lot on the outskirts of town.

from *Verse*

SUSAN WOOD

Gratification

◊   ◊   ◊

You're walking through the woods toward Sepiessa Point,
you and the dog, late September, late afternoon, late light
leafing through its book of trees—pitch pine and beetlebung,
scrub oak, the understory all huckleberry like a good plot,
tangled, dark and bittersweet. You're happy enough,
biding your time. Over there, by Tiah's Cove,
some farmer staked his happiness. See,
even his fence extends a foot or two into the water
to keep his goats from drowning. From a high pole,
an osprey jumps feet first into the cove like a kid
jumping off the high board for the first time. And suddenly,
the trees fall off, the sand plain opens up and there it is,
Tisbury Great Pond, and beyond it,
the Atlantic, going who knows where, and the water
is an improbable blue, like the blue in the windows
at Chartres, a blue no one has ever been able
to reproduce, but here it is. You can barely see
what keeps them apart, the pond
and the ocean, but there in the distance
is a little strip of beach. And sometimes it wears away,
or someone digs it out, and the ocean
enters the pond at last. In the deep sand,
Cosmo the pug staggers like a happy drunk, charges
the water, eyes the merganser rasping
his old smoker's croak. Every time, arriving here
is a surprise, like getting what you've always wanted
but never thought you'd have—the last piece
of peach pie, all the first editions of your favorite writer—
not to sell, just to keep—that longed-for kiss, someone

knowing, *really knowing*, just how you feel. Now
the sun is going down in flames like a ship
on fire, but slowly, listing a little to the left.
Don't worry, everyone on board gets off.
That's the best part. Everyone is saved.

from *Five Points*

FRANZ WRIGHT

A Happy Thought

◇   ◇   ◇

Assuming this is the last day of my life
(which might mean it is almost the first),
I'm struck blind but my blindness is bright.

Prepare for what's known here as death;
have no fear of that strange word *forever.*
Even I can see there's nothing there

to be afraid of: having already been
to forever I'm unable to recall
anything that scared me, there, or hurt.

What frightened me, apparently, and hurt
was being born. But I got over that
with no hard feelings. Dying, I imagine,

it will be the same deal, lonesomer maybe,
but surely no more shocking or prolonged—
It's dark as I recall, then bright, so bright.

from *Field*

ROBERT WRIGLEY

Religion

◊   ◊   ◊

The last thing the old dog brought home
from her pilgrimages through the woods
was a man's dress shoe, a black, still-shiny wing tip.

I feared at first a foot might be in it.
But no, it was just an ordinary shoe.
And while it was clear it had been worn,

and because the mouth of the dog—
a retriever skilled at returning ducks and geese—
was soft, the shoe remained a good shoe,

and I might have given it
to a one-legged friend,
but all of them dressed their prostheses too,

so there it was. A rescued
or a stolen odd shoe. Though in the last months
of the dog's life, I noticed

how the shoe became her friend, almost,
something she slept on or near
and nosed whenever she passed,

as though checking it to see if,
in her absence, that mysterious, familiar,
missing foot might not have come again.

from *The Gettysburg Review*

The Call

◇   ◇   ◇

The call comes and you're out. When you retrieve
the message and return the call, you learn
that someone you knew distantly has died.
His bereaved partner takes you through the news.

She wants to tell you personally how
he fought and, then, how suddenly he went.
She's stunned, and you feel horrible for her,
though somewhat dazed, since he was not a friend,

just someone you saw once or twice a year,
and who, in truth, always produced a shudder:
you confess that you never liked him much,
not to her, of course, but silently to yourself.

You feel ashamed, or rather think the word
ashamed, and hurry off the line. That's when
the image of him appears more vividly,
with nicotine-stained fingertips and hair

like desert weeds fetched up on chicken wire,
the rapacious way he always buttonholed
you at a launch, his breath blowsy with wine.
Well, that will never ever happen again:

one less acquaintance who stops to say hello,
apparently happy at the sight of you.
So why then this surprising queasiness,
not of repulsion but of something like remorse

that comes on you without your guessing it,
till the thing that nagged you most—his laugh, perhaps—
becomes the very music that you miss,
or think you do, or want to, now he's gone.

from *New England Review*

Clam Ode

◇　◇　◇

One attempts to be significant on a grand scale
in the knock-down battle of life
but settles.
I love the expression "happy as a clam,"
how it imparts buoyant emotion
to a rather, when you get down to it,
nonexpressive creature: In piles of ice
it awaits its doom pretty much the same
as on the ocean's floor it awaits
life's banquet and bouquet and sexual joys.
Some barnacles we know are eggs dropped from outer space
but clams, who has a clue how they reproduce?
By trading clouds?
The Chinese thought them capable of prolonging life
while clams doubtlessly considered
the Chinese the opposite.
I remember the jawbreakers my dad would buy me
on the wharf at Stone Harbor,
every thirty seconds you'd take out
the one you were working on
to check what color it turned.
What does this have to do with clams?
A feeling.
States of feeling, unlike states of the upper Midwest,
are difficult to name.
That is why music was invented,
which caused a whole new slue of feelings
and is why ever since
people have had more feelings than they know what to do with

so you can see music sorta backfired
like a fire extinguisher that turns out to be a flame thrower.
They look somewhat alike, don't they?
If you're buying one be sure
you don't get the other,
the boys in the stockroom are stoners
who like to wear their pants falling down
and deserve their own island in *Gulliver's Travels.*
The clam however remains calm.
Green is the color of the kelp it rests on,
having a helluva wingding calm.
I am going to kill you in butter and white wine
so forgive me, great clam spirit,
join yourself to me through the emissary
of this al dente fettuccini
so I may be qualmless and happy as you.

from *POOL*

CONTRIBUTORS' NOTES AND COMMENTS

KIM ADDONIZIO was born in Washington, D.C., in 1954. She is the author of four books of poetry, most recently *What Is This Thing Called Love* (W. W. Norton, 2004) and *Tell Me* (BOA Editions, 2000). Her other books include *The Poet's Companion: A Guide to the Pleasures of Writing Poetry* (W. W. Norton, 1997), with Dorianne Laux; and a novel, *Little Beauties* (Simon & Schuster, 2005).

Of "Verities," Addonizio writes: "One day it struck me that many of the proverbs I was familiar with were reassuring, and that the world—the world I was obsessing over by virtue of paying too much attention to the news—was anything but. So that was the starting point. Cycles of aggression, contradictory truths that lead to the stories we tell to justify what we do. Beliefs about the nature of the world and reality. The moments in life that are unmitigated, unrelieved—the death of hope, I suppose. Those were some of the things I was thinking about."

DICK ALLEN was born in Troy, New York, in 1939, and grew up in the Adirondack foothills village of Round Lake. In 2001, he left an endowed lifetime appointment as a professor and director of a creative writing program in order to devote himself full-time to poetry. He continues to do that, as well as follow long-delayed listening interests in country music (chiefly bluegrass) and classical baroque. With his wife, the poet L. N. Allen, each year he drives around America for a month or so, traveling over ten thousand miles to search for poems. A self-described reclusive "semi-Buddhist," Allen lives with many statues of the Buddha and some twelve-thousand-odd books in a small cottage near Connecticut's Thrushwood Lake. He is the author of seven poetry collections, most recently *The Day Before: New Poems* (2003) and *Ode to the Cold War: Poems New and Selected* (1997), both from Sarabande Books.

Of "'See the Pyramids Along the Nile,'" Allen writes: "Like many others, I often wake up with phrases from poems or songs in my head:

'Death is the mother of beauty,' 'All the sweet green icing,' 'Earth's the right place for love,' 'Just another guy on the lost highway' . . . One morning it was 'See the pyramids along the Nile,' a phrase from the song 'You Belong to Me,' written by Pee Wee King, Chilton Price, and Redd Stewart, and made famous by singer Patsy Cline. All day, the phrase went into and out of my head. At last, I began to understand I was being told that my wandering was going to come to an end soon. I'll never 'see the pyramids along the Nile' in person. As the poem commenced, I found myself trying to capture the bittersweet feelings of doors closing and of nostalgia (without being sentimental; one has to beat back sentimentality in a poem like this) for those early years when all in life seems meadows and blue skies. At the poem's closure, the speaker acknowledges what all of us so often remember and forget: just one different turn among the billion chances and clues and choices of life, and we might have married someone else, lived somewhere else, become someone else; that in the world there are scores of men or women, probably hundreds, thousands, we might have met and lived with had we not chosen to be bound to another—at least on this (yes, a serious pun) plain of our earthly existence.

"The poem incorporates phrases and images from the song. It ultimately seems to me wistful—for the speaker, for the one who wishes him to be loyal to her, and for the one who he might have also loved and who might have loved him. It is the God-given grace of lyric poetry (and song) that it can hold so many complementary and conflicting feelings in the tension of a few allusive words. Anyway, this is what the little phrase that flew into my head one morning finally yielded, after many versions and revisions. I tried to write the poem 'lonesome and blue,' taking my tone from the quiet rhythms of Patsy Cline."

CRAIG ARNOLD was born in California in 1967. His first book, *Shells* (1999), was chosen for the Yale Series of Younger Poets, and his poems have appeared in the 1998 and 2004 editions of *The Best American Poetry.* Awarded the Joseph Brodsky Rome Prize Fellowship by the American Academy of Arts and Letters, he spent a year in Rome working on a "paragraphic novel" inspired by the life and writings of Ovid. In real life, he teaches poetry at the University of Wyoming in Laramie.

Arnold writes: " 'Couple from Hell #11' is the next-to-last passage of a longish poem about the breakdown of a romance—the sort of postmortem that George Meredith performs so gracefully and so bitterly in *Modern Love.* The couple of the poem imagine themselves as Persephone and Hades, playing out the terms of their intimacy, their mutual regrets and recriminations, on the stage of myth. Perhaps we are all, like the Ancient Mariner, bound to rehearse our parts over and over, our dramas growing ever more self-serving and self-regarding. Still, I wanted in this passage to capture that sense of freedom when, however fleetingly, the script slips, and the lines are forgotten, and all at once the self is released into a knowledge of what it is: a limited and mortal body, making its way through the world's beautiful and transparent emptiness. The form of the poem (for readers who share my interest in such things) is a variation on Pindar's three-part ode. His strophes are musical where mine are only palely rhetorical, and I make no claim to the authority of his public, choral voice. I can only wish that this poem's ethical stance—simply enough, that we are not the gods—might have found him not entirely disapproving."

JOHN ASHBERY was born in Rochester, New York, in 1927. He is the author of more than twenty books of poetry, including *Where Shall I Wander* (Ecco/HarperCollins, 2005) and *Chinese Whispers* (Farrar, Straus and Giroux, 2002). His *Selected Prose* was published in 2004 by the University of Michigan Press and by Carcanet in the United Kingdom. Ashbery's *Self-Portrait in a Convex Mirror* (1975) received the Pulitzer Prize, the National Book Critics Circle Award, and the National Book Award. Since 1990 he has been the Charles P. Stevenson, Jr., Professor of Languages and Literature at Bard College. He was guest editor of the inaugural volume of *The Best American Poetry* series in 1988.

"A Worldly Country," which Billy Collins chose for this volume, will be the title poem of Ashbery's collection forthcoming from Ecco next year. Ashbery once remarked that he felt akin to Surrealism "in the same way that the poet Henri Michaux does—he once said that he wasn't a Surrealist, but that Surrealism for him was *la grande permission*—the big permission. The big permission is, I think, as good a definition as any of poetry, of the kind that interests me, at any rate."

JESSE BALL was born on Long Island, New York, in 1978. His first book is *March Book* (Grove Press, 2004). In 2005 he was a Herrick Fellow at Hawthornden Castle in Scotland, and was master poet at the NYHIL poetry festival in Reykjavík, Iceland. He lives in New York and abroad.

Ball writes: "A conversation between a crow and his wife:

"It strikes me foremost that what is wanted in such a knife is delicacy, gentleness, and irresistible sharpness, the delicacy represented in the manner of knowing when, the gentleness in the approach to the coming scene, the target, the environs, the aftermath, and the irresistible sharpness in the darting hand that might once have snatched purses or snapped noses, but that now lays swiftly the substance of the matter like the symmetrical cleaving of a fish that leaves the fish somehow more fishlike than before. Here, then, the keys of permission, to be distributed almost at random. There are often considerations of relative merit, but they grow clear and weak with time. I cannot agree that the oak, for instance, is the best tree for perching. Many maintain, and I will not contradict them, that the sycamore holds pride of place. Surely, what is most needed is a vantage point from which the westward-tending travelers may be observed in their listless momentums. Sometimes one is found resembling the misfortune of a basket. Who, then, is to be blamed?

"But certainly, there is the line of flashing scythes to be considered, and how they pause at midday to retreat to the shade of trees. There we whisper our hopes down from the branches, and often, yes, often, we are obeyed. Whether with or without the one to whom we speak, the leaves fall, the grain exists, does not, rises beneath the sun's teaching hand. All those who resort to the sun can be grouped together and dismissed, if such is your will."

KRISTA BENJAMIN was born in Truckee, California, in 1970, and grew up at Lake Tahoe with her extended family, which owned and operated a resort motel. A 1992 graduate of the University of California, San Diego, she became a schoolteacher, with the intention of writing in the evenings and during vacations. Ten years later, having managed to keep a journal and publish a couple of guest commentaries in a local newspaper, she left the classroom in order to write full-time. She lives in Carson City, Nevada, with her two cats, and is working on a novel.

Of "Letter from My Ancestors," Benjamin writes: "Recently, I helped my grandparents organize the piles of loose photographs they had, including pictures of their parents, grandparents, and other relatives. I heard about my ancestors' lives in Lithuania, Germany, and Austria, and how those who emigrated made their way in the United States.

"When the phrase that became the poem's title came to my mind, I thought about what my ancestors would want to say to me. I doubt it would have occurred to them to write to an unknown great-great-grandchild; they didn't write such 'musings,' as far as I know, although a couple of diaries of the kind mentioned in the poem have survived. But I believe they would be glad to know I am doing work that I love and that I don't have to spend the hours they did in the fields, the post office, or the shop in order to survive."

ILYA BERNSTEIN was born in 1971 in Moscow, then part of the Soviet Union. His poetry collection is called *Attention and Man* (Ugly Duckling Presse, 2003). He works as a translator and lives in New York City.

Of "You Must Have Been a Beautiful Baby," Bernstein writes: "This poem is about Lenny Schlossberg, an actual person. When I showed it to him, he looked skeptical and said, 'This is what passes for poetry nowadays?'"

GAYLORD BREWER was born in Louisville, Kentucky, in 1965. He is a professor at Middle Tennessee State University, where he founded and edits *Poems & Plays*. The most recent of his six books of poetry are *Barbaric Mercies* (Red Hen, 2003), *Exit Pursued by a Bear* (Cherry Grove, 2004), and a collection of apologias, *Let Me Explain* (Iris, 2006).

Brewer writes: " 'Apologia to the Blue Tit' was written in the summer of 2004, during a residency at Hawthornden Castle in Scotland. One morning, rambling the castle's long, sloping drive and doing whatever necessary to avoid writing that day's poem, I found the tit's small body on the tarmac. I enjoy amateur ornithology, and while I generally prefer my birds alive, an unmarked dead specimen does offer an opportunity for close study. I was intent on the inspection when that car of strangers surprised me, and I was further surprised, and angry at myself, that I felt embarrassed, but I did.

"Two weeks later, within fifty yards of the same spot, I discovered the carcass of a tawny owl, and over a succession of evenings came out after dinner to watch the progress of its consumption, probably by a fox. I was intrigued by the enactment of predator as prey, and one night, after nearly missing a call from my wife while I crouched out there in the reliable gloaming, I had enough for a poem. Ditto the rookery, farther along, that eight years before had filled treetops with eighty or ninety raucous nests but was now deserted. Memory, loss, return. Excellent! So that was a good driveway for bird poems, if not so fortunate, apparently, for birds."

TOM CHRISTOPHER was born in Little Rock, Arkansas, in 1978, but more or less grew up outside Dayton, Ohio. He graduated from the University of Pittsburgh, then worked various jobs, from laboratories to straw-bale house construction, before completing an MFA from the University of North Carolina at Greensboro, where he is now a lecturer. He is poetry editor of the upstart journal *The Backwards City Review*.

Of "Rhetorical Figures," Christopher writes: "This poem was born from one of those classes where there was a little friction between the visiting teacher and the students, and all parties went home slightly insulted and upset. During the class, however, the teacher made use of the figure of the One-Legged Man Standing. I found the image and conceit very striking, and before long I had my own collection of figures for various bizarre rhetorical situations. These figures are insignificant when weighed against the reality of human emotion or experience, but I feel that they recognize their uselessness, which, in my mind, forgives them."

LAURA CRONK was born in New Castle, Indiana, in 1977. She holds a BA from Indiana University and an MFA from the New School, where she currently works on the staff of the graduate writing program.

Of "Sestina for the Newly Married," Cronk writes: "Before my marriage I had been working on a series of what I considered to be very serious-minded poems. Right after the wedding, it was difficult to pick up anything I had started previously. It seemed a good time to try a sestina as it's a fun form that pushes the poet forward and tricks her into writing. It also allows for a kind of address that is private and public at the same time. While discussing one evening if anything could have kept us apart, my husband said that he might not have been able to fall in love with me if I had extra fingers or toes. I was righteously angry, but when that cooled, I could concede that it was a pretty funny thing to say. This poem let me put that topic to rest and also indulge in the topic that I couldn't help being so fascinated by—new marriage."

CARL DENNIS was born in St. Louis, Missouri, in 1939. He has lived for many years in Buffalo, New York, where he is writer-in-residence at the State University of New York. He has written nine books of poetry, most recently *New and Selected Poems 1974–2004* (Penguin, 2004). His previous book, *Practical Gods* (Penguin, 2001), won the Pulitzer Prize for poetry in 2002. "Our Generation" is included in his new book of poems, *Unknown Friends*, to be published by Penguin in 2007.

Dennis writes: " 'Our Generation' comes out of my reaching my mid-sixties and wondering what kind of distinct contribution, if any, my generation has made to the country. In particular, I wondered how well my contemporaries and I have filled the places left by our elders, and what more than filling those places, if anything, might be expected of us."

STEPHEN DOBYNS was born in Orange, New Jersey, in 1941. He has published twelve books of poems, twenty novels, a book of short stories, and a book of essays on poetry: *Best Words, Best Order* (Palgrave, 2003). His most recent book of poems is *Mystery, So Long* (Penguin, 2005); his most recent book of fiction is *Eating Naked* (Picador, 2001). He teaches in the MFA programs of Warren Wilson and Sarah Lawrence colleges, and lives in Westerly, Rhode Island.

Dobyns writes: " 'Toward Some Bright Moment' describes an event that took place much as it is described. I thought about the event for a number of years before writing the poem; I still think about it. The action of the blind woman kicking her dog was private in the world of the woman's own darkness, but it was brutally confrontational to the people who witnessed it, including myself. So the subject of the poem becomes the speaker and his reaction, first his anger and then his rationalizations about doing nothing to stop the woman kicking her dog. It ends up indirectly posing a question about our responsibilities within the world: Do we walk by, pretending something doesn't exist, or do we interfere? It is an old question and often there is no good answer. Since the event seemed confrontational, I tried to make the poem confrontational with staccato phrases, five-beat lines, and a repetition of hard K and T sounds, stripping the language of anything pretty or nice. There is nothing pleasant in the poem; there was nothing pleasant in the event. Fortunately, poetry doesn't need to be pleasant."

DENISE DUHAMEL was born in 1961 in Providence and grew up in Woonsocket, Rhode Island. She was educated at Emerson College (BFA) and Sarah Lawrence College (MFA). Her books include *Two and Two* (University of Pittsburgh Press, 2005), *Mille et un sentiments* (Firewheel Editions, 2005), *Queen for a Day: Selected and New Poems* (University of Pittsburgh Press, 2001), *The Star-Spangled Banner* (Southern Illinois University Press, 1999), and *Kinky* (Orchises Press, 1997). She is an associate professor at Florida International University in Miami.

Of " 'Please Don't Sit Like a Frog, Sit Like a Queen,' " Duhamel writes: "This title came to me as part of an e-mail forwarded by my husband, the Filipino-American poet Nick Carbó. The graffiti, as I understand it, is the Filipino equivalent of 'If you sprinkle when you tinkle . . . '

I was drawn to the fairy-tale aspect of the queen and the frog, as well as the pun of the queen on her throne. I chose to use this line (minus the 'please') as the basis for a villanelle exploring feminine cultural identity."

STEPHEN DUNN was born in Forest Hills, New York, in 1939. He divides his time between western Maryland and southern New Jersey, where he teaches at Richard Stockton College of New Jersey. He is the author of thirteen books of poetry, including *Everything Else in the World* (W. W. Norton, 2006) and *Different Hours* (W. W. Norton, 2000), which was awarded the 2001 Pulitzer Prize.

Of "The Land of Is," Dunn writes: "For a number of years the poem existed in its several recalled or invented episodes. They felt like disparate entities, lacking a fulcrum. When, revising it one day, I came up with the phrase 'the land of is,' the poem found both its title and its hidden concern, and permitted me to arrange and shape it accordingly."

BETH ANN FENNELLY was born in Cranford, New Jersey, in 1971, and grew up in a suburb north of Chicago. She teaches English at Ole Miss and lives in Oxford, Mississippi, with her husband, the novelist Tom Franklin, and their four-year-old daughter and infant son. She has published two books of poetry, *Open House* (Zoo Press, 2002) and *Tender Hooks* (W. W. Norton, 2004) and a book of essays, *Great with Child* (W. W. Norton, 2006). This is her third appearance in *The Best American Poetry*.

Fennelly writes: " 'Souvenir' comes from the French 'to remember,' and when I wrote this poem I was musing on how we think we can choose our souvenirs from a vacation or experience, but in fact they choose us. For what I kept remembering from our anniversary trip to Italy was not the famous sites listed in Frommer's or the romance-on-demand of a gondola ride but falling asleep in a darkened train compartment full of strangers and waking up to find that we were all touching. Such accidental intimacy is exactly the type of thing one usually takes pains to avoid. My solitary enjoyment of it felt illicit somehow.

"I think of 'Souvenir' as a kind of love poem, though certainly not the one I would have imagined writing after such a trip."

MEGAN GANNON was born in Chattanooga, Tennessee, in 1975. Educated at Vassar College and the University of Montana, she spent two years with the Peace Corps in the Gambia. She lives in Prescott, Arizona, where she teaches first-graders.

Gannon writes: "I wrote 'List of First Lines' in Missoula, Montana, in

2002. Then in my last semester of the MFA program, I found I could hardly string two words together, and spent the morning slogging around town trying to find one line that had enough momentum to manifest a poem.

"That fall I had moved in with my then-boyfriend, now-husband, Miles Waggener, who was maddeningly, happily churning out the poems that would fill out his first book. The one-hundred-year-old farmhouse from which he seemed to be sucking all the good poems retained a charmingly anachronistic wood-burning stove squashed in against the dishwasher, and a pantry whose floorboards hid the original cellar stairs.

"When the words 'When the winter sits as if' fluttered in, I hustled across slushy medians to a coffeehouse, only to find that the one line would not carry into a second. Using the same sound palette, I tried again: 'When a wrist gives.' Then nothing. With a vague sense of trying to encapsulate the farmhouse, I decided to follow my ear through as many incomplete lines as it took to generate a poem. To my surprise, the attempts to find a poem became a poem. With the exception of cutting a few lines, I think all that changed from that first draft was 'buckshot-strewn, threw, or through with, this,' because I couldn't stomach the two 'ew's so close together."

AMY GERSTLER was born in 1956 in San Diego, California. She lives in Los Angeles. *Ghost Girl*, her most recent book of poems, was published by Penguin Putnam in 2004. Her previous books include *Medicine* (Penguin, 2000), *Crown of Weeds* (Viking Penguin, 1997), *Nerve Storm* (Viking Penguin, 1993), and *Bitter Angel* (North Point Press, 1990; Carnegie-Mellon University Press, 1997), which won a National Book Critics Circle Award. She teaches in the Bennington Writing Seminars program in Bennington, Vermont, and at Art Center College of Design in Pasadena, California, and works as a freelance journalist.

Of "For My Niece Sidney, Age Six," Gerstler writes: "An astonishing entry in the 1910 *Encyclopedia Britannica* generated this poem. The wonderful writer Judith Moore sent me her complete set of these encyclopedias as a present. They are a treasure trove of odd text, amazing information, beautiful illustrations, and a particular bygone worldview articulated in elegant, somewhat archaic prose. I will always be grateful to her for the mind-boggling surprise of these books, with their endless usefulness in providing poem fodder. The entry that sparked this poem is the one for BOILING TO DEATH, which begins: 'a punishment once common both in England and on the continent. The only extant legislative notice of it in England occurs in an act passed in 1531 during the reign of Henry VIII, providing that convicted poisoners should be boiled to death; it is, however, frequently mentioned earlier as a punishment for coining.' (I assume 'coining' might mean making counterfeit money.) I believe in the poetry of fact, and when I stumbled across this entry, my head spun. I felt both elated and a little ill. How could humans ever have done this, and how could it be matter-of-factly recounted in an encyclopedia? I had been trying to write a poem for my niece for months without getting anywhere. With both Sidney and this strange little entry in mind, I tried to imagine having to explain to a child that people had actually written into law and carried out such horrific and unimaginable punishments. And I wanted to write something for Sidney about the difficulty of growing up and finding one's way in the world, especially if one is shy and bookish, and if one tends to live in one's head to an extreme degree."

SARAH GORHAM was born in Santa Monica, California, in 1954, and to her regret, hasn't been back there since. She is the author of three books of poetry: *The Cure* (Four Way Books, 2003), *The Tension Zone* (Four Way Books, 1996), and *Don't Go Back to Sleep* (Galileo Press, 1989). She is a cofounder of Sarabande Books and serves as its president and editor-in-chief.

Of "Bust of a Young Boy in the Snow," Gorham writes: "On the roof of 107 Water Street in Stonington, Connecticut, there's a generous open deck overlooking the harbor, Long Island Sound, and Napatree Point. The house belonged to James Merrill, and my husband, Jeffrey Skinner, and I were guests there for six months in 2002, as poets-in-residence. A small bust of Merrill as a young boy sits precariously, and unceremoniously, on a waist-high porch wall, with one shriveled plant and a small rusty table nearby. I was struck by this little head, that of the great poet, placed here so carelessly, as if someone had planned a more honorable spot but forgot. In the snow particularly, the bust was both sorry and scary. Thus the poem."

GEORGE GREEN was born in Grove City, Pennsylvania, in 1950. He received an MFA in poetry from the New School and currently teaches at Lehman College, CUNY, in the Bronx. His poems have appeared in the anthologies *Poetry 180* and *180 More*, and in *The Best American Poetry 2005*.

Of "The Death of Winckelmann," Green writes: "Winckelmann was the principal art historian of the Greek Revival and a pioneer in classical archaeology. He started out as a schoolmaster in Seehausen. There, in a dismal cottage at the edge of a churchyard, he steeped himself in Homer and Herodotus. His *History of Ancient Art* made him famous.

"Canova's *Perseus* has been moved into the sculpture court at the Metropolitan Museum. When Perseus was on the balcony, he was visible through the glass door of the main entrance on Fifth Avenue. Looking at the statue from the sidewalk late at night could be entrancing, and Central Park could change into a deep and windswept forest in Arcadia. The Met also has Meng's portrait of Winckelmann reading the 'battered Iliad' that he kept with him until the end."

DEBORA GREGER was born in Walsenburg, Colorado, in 1949. She has published seven books of poetry: *Movable Islands* (Princeton University Press, 1980), *And* (Princeton University Press, 1986), *The 1002nd Night* (Princeton University Press, 1990), *Off-Season at the Edge of the World* (University of Illinois Press, 1994), *Desert Fathers, Uranium Daughters* (Penguin USA, 1996), *God* (Penguin USA, 2001), and *Western Art* (Penguin USA, 2004). Her work has appeared in *Ecstatic Occasions, Expedient Forms*, edited by David Lehman (University of Michigan Press, 1995), and in several volumes of *The Best American Poetry*, including the 1998 anthology, edited by John Hollander.

EAMON GRENNAN was born in Dublin, Ireland, in 1941. At Vassar College, he is the Dexter M. Ferry, Jr., Professor of English. He also teaches occasionally in the creative writing programs of Columbia and New York universities. *Still Life with Waterfall* (Graywolf Press, 2002) won the Lenore Marshall Poetry Prize for 2003. His other collections include *Relations: New & Selected Poems* (1998) and *The Quick of It* (2005), both from Graywolf Press. His translations of *Leopardi: Selected Poems* (Princeton University Press, 1997) won the PEN Award for Poetry in Translation. *Facing the Music: Irish Poetry in the Twentieth Century* (Creighton University Press, 1999) is a collection of his critical essays.

Grennan writes: " 'The Curve' reflects my own interest in getting as close as I can to the physical facts of that odd experience we all have: being in a plane, aware of the astonishing forces at work to get you up in the air, keep you up there, and get you safely down to earth again. On this particular occasion I was struck by the arc of the experience—over which you have no control once it starts—and the shifting perspectives it provides. I'm a nervous flyer, usually bristling with the 'what could happen' aspect of being in the grip of something so powerful and strange and at the same time so ordinary that most of us take it for granted (though I can't ever really do that). I suspect the poem was my way of speaking to my nervousness."

DANIEL GUTSTEIN was born in Cleveland, Ohio, in 1968. He lives in Washington, D.C., where he teaches at George Washington University. In addition to teaching creative writing at three colleges and two arts organizations, he has worked as the editor-in-chief of a science journal, an international economist, a farmhand on a cattle farm, a tae kwon do instructor, a Capitol Hill reporter, a theatre arts educator, and a learning specialist with college students who have disabilities.

Of "Monsieur Pierre est mort," Gutstein writes: "My lawyers assure me that I can comment freely on this poem, seeing as the statute of limitations has run out with regard to the mayhem that I visited on Mademoiselle Torrosian's pet rock, Monsieur Pierre, way back in the early 1980s. It's quite possible that I also got M. Pierre stoned, although some would argue that he was stoned to begin with. He was a very quiet rock. A smooth rock, too: you know, good with the ladies. While I had him, I began to worry when I noticed, day after day, the same car out in front of my house. Inside, a portly man in a three-piece suit ate submarine sandwiches. But he didn't arrest me. He arrested my neighbor instead.

"All kidding aside, I wrote this piece and others while recuperating from a terrible injury in Tucson, Arizona. My dog, The Reverend, slept at my feet while I banged out prose poems. The rule was to write margin-to-margin for precisely one page, no more, no less, and see what I had at the end of the day. The other rule was I had to write at least one joke per piece. The form seems to work for me."

R. S. GWYNN was born in Leaksville, North Carolina, in 1948. He is University Professor of English at Lamar University in Beaumont, Texas. *No Word of Farewell: Selected Poems 1970–2000* was published in 2001 by Story Line Press. In 2004 he received the Michael Braude Award for Light Verse from the American Academy of Arts and Letters.

Gwynn writes: "When I told my wife that I had just written a 26-part, 130-line poem titled 'Sects from A to Z,' the bemused look on her face told me that in her opinion I couldn't have gotten very far into the alphabet, let alone have completed it. 'No,' I said, 'S-E-C-T-S.' I've written formal verse for years, and a lot of it is light verse (whatever that means). But I'd never attempted limericks until this poem, which eventually swelled past its abecedarian organizational scheme into a fairly large stack of alternate versions. It was sad to have to discard the Pentecostals in favor of the Presbyterians, but these are the kinds of sacrifices we learn to make for the sake of Art (who lives around the corner and likes a good laugh)."

RACHEL HADAS was born in New York City in 1948. She is Board of Governors Professor of English at the Newark campus of Rutgers University, where she teaches courses in poetry, children's literature, and mythology. Her books of poetry include *Laws* (Zoo Press, 2004), *Indelible* (Wesleyan University Press, 2001), and *Halfway Down the Hall: New & Selected Poems* (Wesleyan, 1998). She is coediting, for publication by W. W. Norton, an anthology of Greek poetry in translation from Homer. A new book of poems, *The River of Forgetfulness*, is due out in 2006 from David Robert Books; *Classics*, a book of essays, will be published by David Robert Books in 2007.

Hadas writes: " 'Bird, Weasel, Fountain' pays homage to things so familiar they risk invisibility. The poetic trope of apostrophe seems to spill over onto the silent painted bird, stuffed weasel, and sculpted fountain, so that they can, as it were, talk back. The Roerich Museum and the fountain are in my longtime neighborhood on the Upper West Side of Manhattan; the weasel can be found, if you look hard enough, in the extraordinarily rich and varied collection (which includes a flag made of beetles, Jefferson Davis's checkerboard, and, in the summer, fresh wildflowers) in the Fairbanks Museum in St. Johnsbury, Vermont."

MARK HALLIDAY was born in Ann Arbor, Michigan, in 1949. He was a founding member of Rhode Island Feminist Theatre in 1973–75. Since 1996 he has taught in the creative writing program at Ohio University. His books of poems are *Little Star* (William Morrow, 1987), *Tasker Street* (University of Massachusetts Press, 1992), *Selfwolf* (University of Chicago Press, 1999), and *Jab* (University of Chicago Press, 2002).

Of "Refusal to Notice Beautiful Women," Halliday writes: "I am so happily married that I can hardly even remember why I wrote this poem. The speaker must be a persona. I wish him luck in his arduous pursuit of maturity; and I'm sure my wife does too."

JIM HARRISON was born in Grayling, Michigan, in 1937. His most recent book is the novella collection *The Summer He Didn't Die* (Atlantic Monthly Press, 2005). His other books include four volumes of novellas (*The Beast God Forgot to Invent*, *Legends of the Fall*, *The Woman Lit by Fireflies*, and

Julip) and eight novels (*True North, The Road Home, Wolf: A False Memoir, A Good Day to Die, Farmer, Warlock, Sundog,* and *Dalva*). The most recent of his seven collections of poetry are *Saving Daylight* (2006) and *The Shape of the Journey: New and Collected Poems* (2000), both from Copper Canyon Press. He collaborated with Ted Kooser on *Braided Creek* (Copper Canyon, 2003). His work has been translated into twenty-five languages. Jim Harrison divides his time between Montana and the Mexican border.

Of "On the Way to the Doctor's," Harrison writes: "This poem was written in a fevered state during a severe illness. I had become intrigued by the organically surreal aspects of being this sick. Every poet loves fresh material, no matter how dire the straits."

ROBERT HASS was born in San Francisco, California, in 1941. His books of poetry include *Sun Under Wood: New Poems* (Ecco Press, 1996), *Human Wishes* (Ecco, 1989), and *Field Guide* (1973), which Stanley Kunitz selected for the Yale Younger Poets Series. Hass served as Poet Laureate of the United States from 1995 to 1997 and is currently a Chancellor of the Academy of American Poets. He edited *The Essential Haiku: Versions of Basho, Buson, and Issa* (Ecco, 1994) and wrote *Twentieth-Century Pleasures: Prose on Poetry* (1984), which won the National Book Critics Circle Award for criticism. He teaches at the University of California, Berkeley, and was guest editor of *The Best American Poetry 2001*.

Of "The Problem of Describing Color," Hass writes: "I remember once, working with Robert Pinsky on the translation of some rhymed poems of Czeslaw Milosz, he remarked that we were having trouble with one particular stanza because 'foot' did not rhyme with 'grass' in English. It seemed a profound observation at the time. The problem with describing color is that a color is not a word. Hence this poem."

CHRISTIAN HAWKEY was born in 1969 on Mars. He is the author of this note as well as of *The Book of Funnels* (Wave Books, 2004) and *HourHour* (Delirium Press, 2005). He lives in Fort Greene, Brooklyn.

TERRANCE HAYES was born in Columbia, South Carolina, in 1971. He is the author of *Wind in a Box* (Penguin, 2006), *Hip Logic* (Penguin, 2002), and *Muscular Music* (Carnegie-Mellon University Contemporary Classics Series, 2005; Tia Chucha Press, 1999). He is a Professor of English at Carnegie-Mellon University in Pittsburgh, where he lives with his wife, the poet Yona Harvey, and their two children.

Of "Talk," Hayes writes: "I have to thank Tony Hoagland for this poem. The years he lived in Pittsburgh we talked often about race and gender and family—subjects people, especially men, rarely discuss intimately and honestly. Having played basketball from middle school through college, I grew up in close contact with white boys. I realized how comfortable I was around my white peers and how comfortable they were around me—and how little we acknowledged the dynamics of race: the clutch of race, the stranglehold just beneath the skin. Not talking about it (race, difference, history) made it seem that integration had succeeded and MLK's dream had come true. Tony made me want to tackle the subject via the kind of rhetorical voice he often uses in his poems. I was hoping for a poem that could be both political and vulnerable—words that often cancel each other out."

BOB HICOK was born in Grand Ledge, Michigan, in 1960. He teaches creative writing at Virginia Tech University. *This Clumsy Living*, his fifth book, will be published by the University of Pittsburgh Press in 2007.

Of "My career as a director," Hicok writes: "A poet goes to a movie. In a plural mood, the poet writes a poem about going to the movies. The poem is published in a respected literary journal and selected by a famous poet for inclusion in a yearly anthology, which is thought by some to be one of the highlights of the season and by others to be a sign of what is wrong with the American temperament. This debate stems largely from the presence of the word 'Best' in the title of the anthology and the fact that poets are largely competing for thimbles. As part of appearing in the anthology, the poet is asked to offer a few comments about his poem. While the poet has enjoyed reading the comments of other poets over the years, he realizes that, of all the things he's not interested in, his thoughts and feelings about his poem are at the top of that list. If he is honest, and the poet likes to think of himself as honest, even as he shoplifts, when he takes only what he honestly needs, he would have to admit, among his other thoughts or feelings, that he prefers watching a movie, pretty much any movie, to writing about his poem about going to the movies. He would have to admit that he is a visual creature; time could be saved if a television were bolted to his face. None of which he wants to admit, being more and more a private person, a person most at ease in the dark, his eyes and skin touched by light in a way that is sexual and not sexual. In particular, this last part is something the poet has no intention of sharing, not ever, not with you."

KATIA KAPOVICH was born in Kishinev, Moldova, on June 21, 1960, the day Russian cosmonaut Yuri Gagarin became the first man to orbit Earth. A bilingual poet writing in English and Russian, Kapovich has written five collections of Russian poetry, including *Veselyi Distsiplinarii* ("Merry Disciplinarian"), which was published in Moscow in 2005. Her collection of English-language poetry is *Gogol in Rome* (Cambridge, U.K.; Salt, 2004). She belonged to a literary dissident movement, emigrated from the Soviet Union in 1990, and now lives in Cambridge, Massachusetts, where she is coeditor of the journal *Fulcrum*.

Of "The Ferry," Kapovich writes: "Two things occur to me in relation to the genesis of this poem. My first recollection relates to our family summer sea trip from Odessa to Crimea. I had just turned three and was allowed aboard the steamer *Rossiia* for free, as if there were little difference between me and a piece of luggage. Fortunately, a big storm on the second day of the journey worked as a source of physical enlightenment. Ever since then, ships, boats, ferries, neumaticos, et al., have fascinated me. The second stimulus comes from my adult observation of the fact that a ghostly 'ship verse' occurs in many wonderful poets. The homemade belief in a 'ship verse' as a litmus for mastership (the way 'exegi monumentum' was for the classical era) grew on me after I challenged myself to put together fifteen to twenty of my favorite contemporary poems in several languages, and discovered that the theme or metaphor of a 'ship' sailed through them. I'd like someday to edit and publish an anthology of ship poems."

LAURA KASISCHKE was born in Lake Charles, Louisiana, in 1961. She has written six books of poetry, most recently *Gardening in the Dark* (Ausable Press, 2004) and *Dance and Disappear* (University of Massachusetts Press, 2002), as well as four novels. A new novel, *Be Mine*, is forthcoming from Harcourt. She teaches at the University of Michigan, and lives with her husband and son in Chelsea, Michigan.

Of "At Gettysburg," Kasischke writes: "My son became obsessed with the Civil War when he was six, and spent a few years dressed as a Union soldier. His knowledge of both the important historical facts and the trivia of the Civil War grew rapidly, and we eventually attended every possible reenactment and visited every monument available to us in Michigan. In the summer of 2005, when he was nine, we fulfilled his dream of going to Gettysburg. The poem, written a week after that visit, is a response to the intensity of his joy upon visiting this battlefield. And my own bafflement. My fear. A mother's despair over a young boy's wild love of war. It is the distance between us, a bloody creek between my devotion to him and his own devotions. But I am also up to my neck in that bloody creek, and aware of the other mothers for whom that place became the most sacred and most profane of all places. Which one of us, I wondered, does not truly understand the nature of war?"

JOY KATZ was born in Newark, New Jersey, in 1963. She lives in Brooklyn with her husband and small dog. She is the author of *The Garden Room* (forthcoming from Tupelo Press in 2006) and *Fabulae* (Southern Illinois University Press, 2002).

Of "Just a second ago," Katz writes: "I've wondered if a stronger version of this poem might be to toss my glass of wine at someone in the first row in the middle of a reading. But please don't sit too far back at my reading. I love you, and I know that version of the poem is juvenile and lazy.

"Some years ago, I was talking to a friend about these absurd urges, random feelings of violence emptied of content, and he said, 'What are you talking about?' The possibility for ruination and hurt is there every second. Yet my friend had never felt such impulses. Maybe that is an even more shocking fact than the unbearable fragility of love and order and being alive in a world that is always so close to flying apart."

DAVID KIRBY was born in Baton Rouge, Louisiana, in 1944. He is the Robert O. Lawton Distinguished Professor of English at Florida State University. His recent books include *The Ha-Ha* (Louisiana State University Press, 2003) and *I Think I Am Going to Call My Wife Paraguay: Selected Early Poems* (Orchises Press, 2004); his next collection will be *The House on Boulevard St.: New and Selected Poems* (Louisiana State University Press). A lot of his poems are set in Europe because often that's the only place where he can find the time to write them. Many refer to his wife, poet Barbara Hamby, his steadfast companion in travel, poetry, and other pleasures.

Of "Seventeen Ways from Tuesday," Kirby writes: "It's important for a poet to be literal-minded, the way a child is. If I had dismissed my fellow museumgoer's comment to his girlfriend by saying, 'Oh, he's probably talking about sex stuff,' I would have missed the opportunity to play with language the way painters amuse themselves with oils and lovers with buttons, hooks, zippers, lips, earlobes, and locks of hair (and that's just for starters). When you're a grown-up, sometimes you forget how to play. So in this poem, I get to be both the kid who asks the question—

'What did he mean when he said that, Dad?'—and the adult who answers it."

JENNIFER L. KNOX was born in 1968 and raised in Lancaster, California, where the wind blows 100 m.p.h. all year long, which is good because it cleans the trash off the side of the road. Her first book, *A Gringo Like Me*, was published by Soft Skull Press (2005). Her work has appeared in the 2003 and 1997 editions of this anthology, as well as the anthologies *Great American Prose Poems: From Poe to the Present* (Scribner, 2003) and *Free Radicals: American Poets Before Their First Book*, edited by Jordan Davis and Sarah Manguso (Subpress, 2004).

Of "The Laws of Probability in Levittown," Knox writes: "A poem doesn't usually 'unlock itself' for me until it has two ideas working inside it. Preferably the two ideas are as different as possible: Swedish meatballs and an angora sweater, frozen blood and a hot air balloon ride, et cetera. So I'd been trying to write a poem using the fish-equals-microfiche factoids for a while, as well as a poem about therapists. Then I put the two together.

"Many cultures believe that poets act as conductors for messages from the dead, or some other kind of spirit—angels, whatever. I'm pretty sure that someone or something else snuck in and wrote the last two lines of the poem. But it's not the first time. It feels like that Daffy Duck cartoon where a giant animator's hand keeps drawing him into goofy outfits, making him do humiliating things against his will. 'I demand to know . . . whoth rethponthible for thith!'"

RON KOERTGE was born in Olney, Illinois, in 1940, and attended the University of Illinois (BA) and the University of Arizona (MA). He taught English and writing at the city college in Pasadena, California, for thirty-seven years and retired in 2001. After publishing half a dozen books with very small presses, Miller Williams, then with the University of Arkansas Press, released three of Koertge's books: *Life on the Edge of the Continent* (1982), *Making Love to Roget's Wife* (1997), and *Geography of the Forehead* (2000). His newest book of poems is *Fever* (Red Hen Press, 2006). Somewhere along the way he found that he could also write novels for teenagers. Best-known of these are *The Arizona Kid*, *Stoner & Spaz*, *The Brimstone Journals*, and *Margaux with an X*, all from Candlewick Press. Koertge loves to bet on thoroughbred racehorses and will go almost anywhere in any weather to cash a ticket.

Of "Found," Koertge writes: "The man in this gratitude poem (Gee,

I wonder who he is?) chastens himself for his restless selfishness until he remembers how much of his well-being he owes to his wife. That's what the poem says. If it means more than that, I leave it to people taller and chalkier than I.

"I do know this much: Without the last stanza, 'Found' is not much more than a valentine. I remember fretting about this until I saw a very slick gambler getting out of a Lincoln at Santa Anita Race Track. Immediately I thought, 'Aha!' And I wrote a note to myself on the back of my racing form.

"Now I (oh, all right, the poem is about me) can be grateful but not uxorious, balancing my wife's generous nature with some unrepentant vanity."

JOHN KOETHE was born in San Diego, California, on December 25, 1945, and graduated from Princeton and Harvard universities. His seven poetry books include *Falling Water* (1997), which received the Kingsley Tufts Award, *North Point North: New and Selected Poems* (2002), and most recently *Sally's Hair* (2006), all from HarperCollins. He is also the author of *Scepticism, Knowledge, and Forms of Reasoning* (2005) and *The Continuity of Wittgenstein's Thought* (1996), both from Cornell University Press. He is Distinguished Professor of Philosophy at the University of Wisconsin, Milwaukee.

Koethe writes: " 'Sally's Hair' was the first of a group of recollective poems I've written over the last few years and which make up the last section of my most recent book, of which it's the title poem. The poem is pretty much self-explanatory: the intense blue and gold colors of a summer day made me remember a woman I met when I was a junior in college, and I simply wrote the encounter down. Some of the other poems in the group are centered upon memories of a track meet in high school, reading through all of *Remembrance of Things Past* (appropriately enough), watching Secretariat win the Triple Crown in 1973, and seeing Richard Burton portray Hamlet when I was a college freshman. I had a lot of fun writing them."

MARK KRAUSHAAR was born in 1945, grew up in Concord, Massachusetts, and attended Marlboro College in Vermont. Afterward he briefly taught high school, drove a taxi in Boston, worked in a factory in England, and clerked at a motel desk in Cambridge, Massachusetts. He has also worked as a wig salesman in Kentucky, a pipe welder in southern Mississippi, and, for the past twenty-two years, a psychiatric nurse in Madison,

Wisconsin. His poems have been anthologized in *Motion: American Sports Poems* (University of Iowa Press, 2001) and *Visiting Walt: Poems Inspired by the Life and Work of Walt Whitman* (Iowa, 2003).

Of "Tonight," Kraushaar writes: "The poem is a pretty nearly literal account of an evening spent thinking, trying not to think, of a friend's newly diagnosed cancer. It struck me, as I think it does many people, how utterly arbitrary and unfair it seemed, and is, and I began the poem lying on a green sofa and watching a terribly sad and perfectly pointless police reality television show just as the poem says. I can't remember about the dime now, but there was an opened magazine and trucks and the neighbor's inevitable barking dog.

"My friend, I'm happy to say, is confounding the doctors and doing splendidly."

JULIE LARIOS was born in Ellensburg, Washington, in 1949. She grew up in the Bay Area and now lives in Seattle. Harcourt recently published her third picture book, *Yellow Elephant*, a book of poetry for children, illustrated by artist Julie Paschkis.

Of "Double Abecedarian: Please Give Me," Larios writes: "I first encountered double abecedarians a few years ago, and since then I've been smitten by the structural bravado of the form. They remind me of old wooden roller coasters—a bit rickety, not completely graceful, but full of speed and pleasure and quick changes in direction. Going through the alphabet from A to Z at the beginning of lines, and Z to A at the end of lines, double abecedarians respond to Robert Frost's often-quoted advice that poets working outside of form are like people playing tennis without a net. Here, the net is not only up, but the boundary lines have been laid out full court, and within those lines an energetic game is played. It's interesting to take language down to sentence sounds, then down again to word and syllable sounds, until we get to the alphabet, each letter with its own charms. So 'Please Give Me' is an alphabetical rant about Freudians. Freud's ideas, which are more subtle than their now-accepted representations, can be misused by people who press emotional grids down over the physical landscape of objects. Since few things on the planet are perfectly flat, the idea that male (convex) and female (concave) properties can be assigned to all objects we think about is a bit daft. And the resulting theory, which assumes that thoughts about three-dimensional objects are to be interpreted as the sexual preoccupations of distressed people, strikes me as cruel, shallow, simple-minded, and lacking nuance. Or hoopla, as the poem says."

DORIANNE LAUX was born in Augusta, Maine, in 1952. She grew up in Southern California and in the early 1980s moved to the Bay Area, where she attended Mills College in Oakland. Her books include *Smoke* (2000), *What We Carry* (1994), and *Awake* (BOA Editions, 1990). She is also coauthor, with Kim Addonizio, of *The Poet's Companion: A Guide to the Pleasures of Writing Poetry* (W. W. Norton, 1997). Norton recently published her fourth book of poems, *Facts About the Moon*. She teaches in the creative writing program at the University of Oregon and lives in Eugene with her husband, the poet Joseph Millar, and her daughter, Tristem.

Laux writes: " 'Demographic' was a poem I took out of the manuscript of *Facts About the Moon* in the final hour. It was still included in the galleys. I decided the poem was too similar in theme to another poem in the book, 'Democracy,' also about boarding and riding a bus. These days, the bus is where I get many of my poems written, since it is one of the few stretches of time when I'm free from the phone, the computer, students, family. I will often make quick character sketches of the people around me that will later turn themselves into full poems. This particular piece focuses on those who are encumbered by life's bodily disasters and have to make their way around the world the same as any able-bodied individual but with a complex set of obstacles and adjustments. I'm amazed again and again by the patience of these people as well as the other riders and the bus drivers. It's sometimes a community effort to get just one person on the bus and settled for the short ride to the grocery store, the hospital, or the university. Maybe the bus is one of the last bastions of humanity and democracy. I've noticed that I have begun to feel a great sense of calm and comfort fall over me as soon as I reach the stop and sit down among my comrades on the metal bench. Every age, sex, race, and class is represented there and I know what my role is, what is expected of me as a member of this movable and intimate society. We wave to one another, greeting each other by name, making room in the seat next to us or standing up for the elderly or infirm. For once, we all know who we are and where we're going, and we have one another to help us get there."

REB LIVINGSTON was born in Pittsburgh, Pennsylvania, on Christmas Day, 1972. She is the author of *Pterodactyls Soar Again* (Whole Coconut Chapbook Series, 2006) and an editor of *No Tell Motel* (www.notellmotel.org) and the anthology *The Bedside Guide to No Tell Motel* (No Tell Press, 2006). She lives in northern Virginia with her husband and son.

Livingston writes: " 'That's Not Butter' is loosely based on Little Black

Sambo, a once-popular children's story no longer taught due to its offensive racial characterizations. Few people my age are familiar with the story or its history, although my kindergarten teacher read it to our class. As young children oblivious to British imperialism, we loved the tale because to us it was about pancakes and a little boy who outsmarted tigers. In the summer of 2004, I spent most of my time lying on the sofa, suffering from all-day morning sickness. Pregnancy gave too much time to ponder the innocence of childhood and obsess about what kind of devil-child I would soon bring into the world. That same summer, Shafer Hall put out a call on his blog for 'tiger' poems. Sambo was on my mind, and so I wrote."

THOMAS LUX was born in Northampton, Massachusetts, in 1946. He is the Bourne Professor of Poetry at the Georgia Institute of Technology. His most recent book is *The Cradle Place* (Houghton Mifflin, 2004).

Lux writes: "I think of 'Eyes Scooped Out and Replaced by Hot Coals' as an audience participation poem, i.e., readers may replace the book mentioned in the poem with a beloved book of their choice."

PAUL MULDOON was born in County Armagh, Northern Ireland, in 1951, and educated in Armagh and at the Queen's University of Belfast. From 1973 to 1986 he worked in Belfast as a radio and television producer for the British Broadcasting Corporation. Since 1987 he has lived in the United States, where he is now Howard G. B. Clark '21 Professor in the Humanities at Princeton University. Between 1999 and 2004 he was Professor of Poetry at the University of Oxford. Paul Muldoon's main collections of poetry are *New Weather* (1973), *Mules* (1977), *Why Brownlee Left* (1980), *Quoof* (1983), *Meeting the British* (1987), *Madoc: A Mystery* (1990), *The Annals of Chile* (1994), *Hay* (1998), *Poems 1968–1998* (2001), *Moy Sand and Gravel* (2002), and *Horse Latitudes* (2006). He was guest editor of *The Best American Poetry 2005*.

Muldoon writes: "'Blenheim' is one of a sequence of nineteen sonnets brought together under the general title 'Horse Latitudes.' Each sonnet is named after a battle in which horses, or mules, played a major role, and began as a response to the Bush regime's disastrous incursion into Iraq. The Battle of Blenheim was fought on August 13, 1704, between a confederation of English and Austrian forces, led by the Duke of Marlborough, and a confederation of French and Bavarians. While it's hard to read this sonnet out of context, one might point to the phrase 'those weeks and months in the doldrums,' which refers to the main sense of

'Horse Latitudes' as that area between the tropics in which sailing ships were often becalmed. In an effort to lighten the ships, horses were sometimes pitched overboard. Expendability, of troops and truth, might be said to be a subject of the larger sequence. An Iron Maiden is an instrument of torture. Mummichog and menhaden are two types of fish, the former a small mullet, the latter a herring. The name menhaden comes, it seems, from a Narragansett word having to do with enriching, or fertilizing, land."

MARILYN NELSON was born in Cleveland, Ohio, in 1946, and grew up on military bases in various places in the United States. She holds a BA from the University of California, Davis, an MA from the University of Pennsylvania, and a PhD from the University of Minnesota. Her major publications are *For the Body* (1978), *Mama's Promises* (1985), *The Homeplace* (1990), *Magnificat* (1994), *The Fields of Praise: New and Selected Poems* (1997), and *The Cachoiera Tales and Other Poems* (2005), all published by Louisiana State University Press; *Carver: A Life in Poems* (2001) and *Fortune's Bones: The Manumission Requiem* (2005), both published by Front Street Books; and *A Wreath for Emmett Till* (Houghton Mifflin, 2005). She has translated a play by Euripides (*Hecuba*) and the work of two Danish poets, Halfdan Rasmussen and Inge Pedersen. Nelson is a professor emerita of English at the University of Connecticut.

Of "Albert Hinckley," Nelson writes: "This sonnet is part of a sequence of twelve that is to be published with a sequence of twelve sonnets by Elizabeth Alexander on the same subject: the short-lived boarding school for 'young ladies of color' opened by Miss Prudence Crandall in the village of Canterbury, Connecticut, in 1833. Teacher and students were harassed; a law was passed to ban the school; Crandall was arrested and jailed; the well was poisoned, the house set on fire. This sonnet is based on two historical facts: a young white man named Albert Hinckley was one of the school's supporters, and the girls' wagon was overturned in a stream after a service at the local abolitionist-leaning Baptist church. The connection, the scene, and the speaker are invented."

RICHARD NEWMAN was born outside Chicago, Illinois, in 1966 and grew up in southern Indiana. He lives in St. Louis, Missouri, where he edits *River Styx*, writes freelance, and teaches at St. Louis Community College. His most recent poetry collections are *Borrowed Towns* (Word Press, 2005) and the chapbook *Monster Gallery: 19 Terrifying and Amazing Monster Sonnets!* (Snark Publishing, 2005).

Of "Briefcase of Sorrow," Newman writes: "If, when I was a student, a writing teacher told me never to write about something (Grandma, poetry, teaching, Oklahoma) or not to write a certain way (formal, narrative, syllabic), my first instinct was always to go home and break the rule—say, a formal poem about Grandma teaching syllabic poetry in Oklahoma. Now a teacher myself, I often use Frances Mayes's *The Discovery of Poetry*, but the first semester I tried that textbook, we came to the 'Six Danger Signals' section about not using the word *of* to name a metaphor, as in *briefcase of sorrow*, and immediately after class I went to my office and wrote the first draft."

MARY OLIVER was born in the Cleveland suburb of Maple Heights, Ohio, in 1935. She has published fifteen books of poetry and five books of prose. *American Primitive* received the Pulitzer Prize in 1984, and *New and Selected Poems* won the National Book Award in 1992. Beacon Press published *New and Selected Poems, Volume Two* in 2005 as well as her first poetry CD, *At Blackwater Pond*, in 2006. She has lived in Provincetown, Massachusetts, for more than forty years. "I still don't do much but write," she reports. "I have had a happy life."

DANIELLE PAFUNDA was born in Albany, New York, in 1977. She is the author of *Pretty Young Thing* (Soft Skull Press, 2005) and coeditor of the online journal *La Petite Zine*. She works on *The Georgia Review* and teaches in the University of Georgia's English Department.

Pafunda writes: " 'Small Town Rocker' has an unfortunately autobiographical engine. I'd like to think that each of us, at some point, falls for a bargain-basement Lizard King. A false Dimitri in the rock-star kingdom."

MARK PAWLAK was born in Buffalo, New York, in 1948. His fifth poetry collection, *Official Versions* (Hanging Loose), in which the poem in this anthology appears, was published earlier this year. His other books include *Special Handling* (Hanging Loose, 1993), *All the News* (Hanging Loose, 1984), and *The Buffalo Sequence* (Copper Canyon, 1976). He has edited four anthologies. He is director of Academic Support Programs at the University of Massachusetts, Boston, where he teaches mathematics. He lives in Cambridge with his wife and his teenage son.

Of "The Sharper the Berry," Pawlak writes: "I take inspiration from the Berlin Dada Manifesto (c. 1920), which stated, in essence, that the artist's task is no longer to represent the world but to rearrange it. Scraps of commonplace language grab my attention and are often the materials from which I fabricate poems—overheard conversation, pop song lyrics, the words of advertising circulars, and news articles, et cetera. When I happened upon a list of well-worn clichés, I found it to be suggestive of a greeting card, which prompted me to splice and arrange the phrases to make this poem, 'The Sharper the Berry.' I hope to interest Hallmark in my handiwork and perhaps, in this way, to supplement my meager income as a poet."

THIEN-BAO THUC PHI was born in Saigon, Vietnam, in 1975, and raised in the Phillips neighborhood of south Minneapolis. On full scholarship, he studied with Diane Glancy at Macalester College. A multiple Minnesota Grand Poetry Slam champion and National Poetry Slam individual finalist, Bao Phi has been a featured performer in venues from the Nuyorican Poets Café to Stanford University. He works at the Loft, a nonprofit literary arts organization, where he created and curates Equilibrium, a spoken word and performance poetry series.

Of "Race," Phi writes: "A few years ago, I was considering how mainstream American culture had grown fascinated by illegal import street racing, a phenomenon started largely by Asian Americans. Predictably, as the mainstream coopted the import racing scene, Asian Americans were largely left out of the picture or relegated to supporting roles. From import tuner television shows to street-racing video games to the Hollywood film *The Fast and the Furious*, Asian Americans were, and continue to be, largely ignored or rendered invisible within the suddenly fashionable and lucrative counterculture that they had created.

"In struggling to capture the many issues of racism, exploitation, and classism that dovetailed when thinking about import tuner culture, I wrote three poems vastly different in tone, voice, and content. I eventually scrapped the other two poems and concentrated on revising and editing the performance poem included here, 'Race.' I wrote it imagining the motor-mouthed narrator to be excitedly telling the story to friends, tripping over his or her own words, and the style of the ending sequence to reflect the car-race metaphor: as the driver shifts gears and the car goes faster, the words and images resemble stream-of-consciousness; the sentences run on, and the narrator spits the words out louder and faster. I'd like to thank those members of the import tuner community who have read the piece and offered constructive criticism and technical expertise that have proved invaluable to my rewrites."

DONALD PLATT was born in Coral Gables, Florida, in 1957. His two books of poetry, both from Purdue University Press, are *Fresh Peaches, Fireworks, & Guns* (1994) and *Cloud Atlas* (2002). His poems are included in *The Best American Poetry 2000* and in the 2003 and 2005 editions of *The Pushcart Prize* annual. An associate professor of English at Purdue University, he lives in West Lafayette, Indiana, with his wife and two daughters.

Platt writes: "The genesis of 'Two Poets Meet' occurred when I happened upon seven sentences from George Starbuck's 1977 interview with Elizabeth Bishop, which Carolyn Forché quotes in her introduction to a selection of Latin American poets in the anthology *The Poetry of Our World*. When Starbuck asked her about Brazilian writers, Bishop responded, 'The one I admire most of the older generation is Carlos Drummond de Andrade. I've translated him. I didn't know him at all. He's supposed to be very shy. I'm supposed to be very shy. We've met once—on the sidewalk at night. We had just come out of the same restaurant, and he kissed my hand politely when we were introduced.' Nowhere else, as far as I know, does Bishop describe this meeting. Completely charmed by her brief description, I immediately started imagining the scene more fully and soon found myself writing this poem. I added Lota de Macedo Soares, Bishop's longtime lover, who would have been the logical person to make the introduction. I reread Bishop's translations of Andrade and consulted a grease-spattered copy of *The New York Times International Cookbook* for details about Brazilian cuisine. The initial draft of the poem took a few days to write and then went through several revisions in the next six months or so.

"However, its theme—how two poets might greet each other with grace, compassion, and respect—is one that I had been trying to write about for a long time. In 1993 I had attended a reading given by Mark Strand and Stanley Kunitz in Salt Lake City. Kunitz, whom I had never heard before, read first and recited many of his greatest hits, as well as the new poems that had been appearing during the preceding year in *The New Yorker*. When Strand got up, he said simply, 'After that reading, I feel like a pixie.' I think he summarized how all of the writers in the audience felt. In 1999 I saw Donald Justice and Edgar Bowers embrace each other before a reading at the Sewanee Writers Conference. Both were in their mid-seventies, and their embrace implied to me, rightly or wrongly, a long friendship and also a recognition of the fact that they might not see each other again. Indeed, Bowers died less than six months later. I wrote a disastrously sentimental villanelle about that moment. These two experiences provided an invisible, but crucial, backdrop to the writing of 'Two Poets Meet.'"

LAWRENCE RAAB was born in Pittsfield, Massachusetts, in 1946. He is the author of six collections of poetry, including *Visible Signs: New and Selected Poems* (2003), *The Probable World* (2000), and *What We Don't Know About Each Other* (1993), all published by Penguin. He lives in Williamstown, Massachusetts, where he teaches literature and writing at Williams College.

Of "The Great Poem," Raab writes: "There's a moment in the making of some poems when it feels like anything is possible. You know you've worked your way into the presence of a genuine poem, but its limitations—of phrasing, of subject, of range—haven't yet revealed themselves. The thrill you feel is of imminence, enormous promise. What you're on the edge of could be better than anything you've written before. It could be the great poem. After all, wasn't every truly great poem preceded by lesser, merely very good poems? And why shouldn't it happen to you, after so many years of practice? Of course, all the poems you've completed argue against it. The pattern of their limitations is cruelly persuasive evidence. Yet breakthroughs happen. Think of May 1819: Keats's 'Ode to a Nightingale.' And that was just the beginning. This sweet illusion is the shadow life behind 'The Great Poem,' which is quick to admit that it is not the great poem, though for a moment its title—now merely playful—might have suggested otherwise."

BETSY RETALLACK was born in 1957 in a rural Maine town called Bethel. Music was her first love. In 2004 her first published poem, "Treasure Box," appeared in the *Endicott Review*. She teaches music in the Beverly, Massachusetts, public schools and lives on Poets Hill with her two grown sons, Kyle and Garth, and her husband, Mark, who was the inspiration for "Roadside Special."

Of "Roadside Special," Retallack writes: "My husband has an eye for what sells on the side of the road, always looking for a good bargain. This is especially true when it comes to large items such as cars and boats. We often owned used cars that did not last very long. But it wasn't just cars, it was also boats. The poem doesn't even mention all the boats we ever owned but merely sidelines the idea. The mention of the canoe conveys some angst concerning the boat purchases as well.

"The crux of the poem seems to be found in the differences in what men and women expect and understand about themselves. The contrast is made blatantly between fruit and cars. Something small and simple is compared to something large and complicated. I actually wouldn't mind trying out the '70 black El Camino."

LIZ ROSENBERG was born in Glen Cove, New York, in 1956. She teaches at the State University of New York at Binghamton, and has published three books of poems, four novels, and more than twenty books for young readers. She writes a monthly book-review column for the *Boston Globe*. Her books include *Children of Paradise* (poems; University of Pittsburgh Press, 1994), *Heart and Soul* (novel; Harcourt Brace, 1996), and *I Just Hope It's Lethal: Poems of Sadness, Madness and Joy*, edited with Deena November (Houghton Mifflin, 2005).

Of "The Other Woman's Point of View," Rosenberg writes: "About this poem I have little to say except that such poems are difficult to write. I think most people who love at all have occasionally loved badly, painfully, and blunderingly. Perhaps this poem will speak to them. I am always interested in the other woman's point of view. History is filled with the silence of women. Part of poetry's task, it may be, is to break that silence, even when painful."

J. ALLYN ROSSER was born in Bethlehem, Pennsylvania, in 1957. Her first collection, *Bright Moves* (Northeastern University Press, 1990), won the Samuel French Morse Poetry Prize. Her second, *Misery Prefigured* (Southern Illinois University Press, 2001), won the Crab Orchard Award. She teaches at Ohio University.

Of "Discounting Lynn," Rosser writes: "People frequently confuse hover flies (diptera), which can't sting, with sweat bees (hymenoptera), because through Batesian mimicry hover flies manage to look more like honey bees than sweat bees do. So you, like the speaker, might have heard that sweat bees aren't really bees. They like to lick sweat from people; they are 'solitary'; the female makes its nest in the ground or in rotting wood, then lays an egg on a pollen ball, seals off the nest, and forgets about it. This is not what one tends to think of as normal bee behavior. Nonetheless officially it is a bee, so the speaker, who in correcting herself mistakes the sweat bee for the hover fly commonly mistaken for the sweat bee, is even more confused than she supposes.

"I think of this poem as a kind of literary panic attack."

KAY RYAN was born in California in 1945 and grew up in the small towns of the San Joaquin Valley and the Mojave Desert. She studied at the Los Angeles and Irvine campuses of the University of California. Since 1971 she has lived in Marin County. She has published six books of poetry, including *Flamingo Watching* (Copper Beech Press, 1994) and *Elephant Rocks* (1996), *Say Uncle* (2000), and *The Niagara River* (2005), all from Grove Press. Her work was included in the 1995, 1999, and 2005 volumes of *The Best American Poetry*, as well as in Harold Bloom's edition of *The Best of the Best American Poetry 1988–1997*. She received the Ruth Lilly Poetry Prize in 2004.

Of "Thin," Ryan writes: "The joke-to-poem ratio here is riskily high. It's still in solution, but it's supersaturated. When you have a case like this, it's not a good idea to jostle it with commentary; the joke can settle out and then you've got a few pallid words with some junk at the bottom."

MARY JO SALTER was born in Grand Rapids, Michigan, in 1954. She is Emily Dickinson Senior Lecturer in the Humanities at Mount Holyoke College and lives in Amherst, Massachusetts. She is coeditor, with Margaret Ferguson and Jon Stallworthy, of *The Norton Anthology of Poetry* (4th ed., 1996, and 5th ed., 2005, both published by W. W. Norton). Her first play, *Falling Bodies*, was produced in 2004, and she has published one children's book, *The Moon Comes Home* (Knopf, 1989). Her five collections of poetry include *Henry Purcell in Japan* (1985), *Unfinished Painting* (1989), *Sunday Skaters* (1994), *A Kiss in Space* (1999), and *Open Shutters* (2003), all from Knopf.

Of "A Phone Call to the Future," Salter writes: "This poem sat on the desk for over a year after I'd written it, because I distrusted the speed with which I wrote it. And yet it crystallizes thoughts I've had for years. It came out in one sitting almost as it remains here. While the poem's rhythm is more iambic than not, it isn't metrical, it has no rhyme scheme, and, in short, it doesn't sound like a poem I'd write—while conscious. It feels still like dream thinking, specifically like the half-waking state in which I found myself staring at a television one night in a motel room in New Hampshire, cutting people off in midsentence and welcoming others in midsentence with my remote control, drifting into and out of sleep. On one channel, cute Sandra Dee (or was it Tuesday Weld?) mugged for the camera at age eighteen or so; on another channel, the same actress was shown seconds later in droopy middle age. This was science fiction; I was science fiction; I—the very notion of an 'I,' along with almost everything else I grew up assuming—was as dated and unreal as the channel-surfed, fast-forwarded Tuesday Weld."

VIJAY SESHADRI was born in India in 1954. He is the author of two books of poems, *Wild Kingdom* and *The Long Meadow*, both from Graywolf Press. He lives in Brooklyn with his wife and son, and teaches poetry and nonfiction writing at Sarah Lawrence College.

Seshadri writes, " 'Memoir' was born in a moment of bemusement about a memoir I have been writing, sporadically, for a while now. I felt that even though I couldn't get untracked writing the prose I could make a poem out of my frustration, which would be about what we do and do not reveal. Friends who have read the poem have read it as a confession of sorts and have commended me for what they see as a new willingness to fess up on my part. Actually, though, the poem is not confessional but is about the art of narrative, at least from my point of view. I've always seen it as a piece of literary criticism."

ALAN SHAPIRO was born in Boston, Massachusetts, in 1952. He teaches at the University of North Carolina at Chapel Hill, where he lives with his wife, Callie Warner, and their three children. Houghton Mifflin published his most recent book of poems, *Tantalus in Love*, in 2005. A volume of his new and selected poems is due out from the same publisher in 2008.

Shapiro writes: " 'Misjudged Fly Ball' was occasioned by the death of my dear friend Timothy Dekin, a wonderful poet who died of a rare lung disorder in 2001."

CHARLES SIMIC was born in Belgrade, Yugoslavia, in 1938. He is a poet, essayist, and translator, and teaches American literature and creative writing at the University of New Hampshire. He has published twenty collections of his own poetry, five books of essays, a memoir, and numerous books of translations. He has won the Pulitzer Prize and a MacArthur Fellowship. *The Voice at 3 A.M.*, a volume of selected and new poems, was published by Harcourt in 2003; *My Noiseless Entourage* followed in spring 2005. His books in the Michigan "Poets on Poetry" series include *The Unemployed Fortune-Teller* (1994), *Orphan Factory* (1997), and *A Fly in the Soup* (2000). He was the guest editor of *The Best American Poetry 1992.*

Of "House of Cards," Simic writes: "This is an early memory. I was born in 1938 in Belgrade, Yugoslavia, and lived there throughout the

Nazi occupation. At night, there were arrests, bombings, and long, tense moments of listening for footsteps in the street. We didn't want to make any noise, so we read, looked at pictures, or played cards."

GERALD STERN was born in Pittsburgh, Pennsylvania, in 1925. His most recent book of poems is *Everything Is Burning* (W. W. Norton, 2004). He is the author of fourteen books of poetry, including *American Sonnets* (2002) and *This Time: New and Selected Poems*, which won the 1998 National Book Award. He was awarded the 2005 Wallace Stevens Award by the Academy of American Poets. He is retired from the University of Iowa Writers' Workshop, where he taught for many years.

Of "Homesick," Stern writes: "My nostalgia is for the life I didn't live in my twenties—which would have been staying in France and working there and falling in love and translating the poets, just as Odysseus's true nostalgia was for the dear life he didn't have with Nausicaa and not the dull life he did have with Penelope. It is also for the life I didn't have as a Moroccan Jew exiled to France in the 1960s, which I became obsessed with after long conversations with a Moroccan friend, Ruth Setton, whose family had to escape quickly. Libby is my beloved grandmother whose photograph, taken in Poland in 1902 when she was thirty-two years old, hangs over my mantle. Her samovar disappeared sixty years ago. Ezra refers to the Jewish scribe, not the American poet. The details (the images) are from the life I lived (and didn't live) during my journey. It's called 'my past.' The last sentence is what Maceo Pavlick de Niord said when he was going on three, four years ago.

"As I grow older I realize more and more how I was part of an extraordinarily large migration, and that I too lined up for my number, and that it will go on."

JAMES TATE was born in Kansas City, Missouri, in 1943. *Return to the City of White Donkeys*, his most recent book of poems, was published by the Ecco Press (HarperCollins) in 2004. Among his other books are *Shroud of the Gnome* (Ecco, 1997); *Worshipful Company of Fletchers* (Ecco, 1994), winner of the National Book Award; and *Selected Poems* (Wesleyan University Press, 1991), which received the Pulitzer Prize. He teaches at the University of Massachusetts in Amherst and was the guest editor of *The Best American Poetry 1997*.

SUE ELLEN THOMPSON was born in New Jersey in 1948. She is the author of *This Body of Silk*, which won the 1986 Samuel French Morse

Prize from Northeastern University Press; *The Wedding Boat* (Owl Creek Press, 1995); *The Leaving: New & Selected Poems* (Autumn House Press, 2001); and *The Golden Hour* (Autumn House Press, 2006). She has taught at Central Connecticut State University, Wesleyan, and Middlebury. She recently edited *The Autumn House Anthology of Contemporary American Poetry.*

Thompson writes: " 'Body English' is one of a series of poems written in the months following my mother's death from cancer in 2002. It was one of the few times in my life when I wrote about a difficult experience while going through it, rather than waiting several months for the memories to settle. The challenge was to avoid indulging my own impulse to grieve over every last detail of her illness and death. In this poem I try to approach that grief indirectly by focusing on a single physical gesture. I also wanted to write about an aspect of death—what happens to the body—that was entirely unfamiliar."

TONY TOWLE was born in Manhattan in 1939 and has lived there most of his life, at present in Tribeca. He became associated with Frank O'Hara, Kenneth Koch, John Ashbery, and the "New York School of Poetry" in 1963. His first major collection was *North*, which received the Frank O'Hara Award for 1970. His other books of poetry and prose, twelve in all, include *The History of the Invitation: New & Selected Poems 1963–2000* and *Memoir 1960–1963.*

Of "Misprision," Towle writes: "This poem got its impetus from e-mail correspondence with the poet Michele Somerville, when she made a remark about Sappho being recited in her original tongue—which stuck with me as an amusingly vague double-entendre that connected with several other notes and sketches I had, and I was eventually inspired to put them together. The last stanza did come last, in this case, and finishes up the concept by taking off into the reaches of metaphysicality. The archaic *misprision*, used here in its sense of 'misunderstanding,' is a word Charles North and I have been using ironically in conversation for many years (decades), and I finally got the opportunity to put it into print."

ALISON TOWNSEND was born in Allentown, Pennsylvania, in 1953, and grew up outside Philadelphia and in rural New York State. Educated at Marlboro College and Vermont College, she is the author of *The Blue Dress* (White Pine Press, 2003) and *What the Body Knows* (Parallel Press, 2002). She lives with her husband on four acres of prairie and oak savanna in the farm country outside Madison, Wisconsin, and teaches English at the University of Wisconsin, Whitewater.

Townsend writes: "The experience described in 'What I Never Told You About the Abortion' was so visceral that it was difficult even to begin to capture in words, though I had wanted to do so for almost twenty years. When the lines eventually came through, they did so with a kind of severity, an almost judicial authority, as if being offered as evidence in court by a witness. When I hit, unconsciously at first, upon the anaphoric repetition of the word *that*, with long lines gathered into couplets, I had a foothold into the poem that allowed me to move from one image to another, navigating the rock wall that grief can sometimes be. As I made my way through the poem, which began as and remains an elegy, I saw it was also an interrogation—of the clinic, the doctor, the narrator and her partner, and their failures at communication. Aesthetic decisions felt dictated almost entirely by subject matter. The poem had to be stark and plain-spoken. It had to be relentless. It had to feel inevitable. And in the end, words had to be incomplete, inadequate. Though they are (to paraphrase Faulkner) all we have."

PAUL VIOLI was born in New York City in 1944 and grew up in Greenlawn, Long Island. His twelfth book of poetry, *Scramble and Glide*, is forthcoming from Hanging Loose Press. Other recent books include *Selected Accidents, Pointless Anecdotes* and *Fracas*, also from Hanging Loose, and a selection of long poems, *Breakers*, from Coffee House Press. He teaches at the New School and at Columbia University.

Of "Counterman," Violi writes: "I can't think of anything to say about the poem itself, so, for what it's worth, I'll resort to recounting what set it off. I'd come across a notebook entry where I'd been playing around with the tempo and diction of a deli-counter dialogue. I hadn't read it in about half a year and didn't think I'd make anything more out of it, but then two incidents clicked in. One was recent. I'd walked into an SRO deli on West Third Street in Manhattan and heard a customer with a very heavy brogue present the following syllogism to a stolid Mexican counterman: 'So you've never been to Ireland then. So you don't know what you're talking about then. So you should shut your mouth then.' They stared at each other in a very hard way and everyone was tense. Then they both cracked up laughing. Apparently this was a little routine they did every day. The other incident occurred in a Hoboken deli more than twenty years before that. A taciturn, solemn counterman took my order and proceeded to fill it with great care and deliberation that seemed to say that each and every sandwich he made was the Perfect Sandwich. He said not a word and served it with an attitude that was a blend of dignity and disdain. Anyway, even though the poem doesn't retain the tone of either of those recollections, once they came into play I quickly added the second interchange to the notebook dialogue."

ELLEN BRYANT VOIGT was born in 1943 in Pittsylvania County, Virginia, where she grew up. She has published six volumes of poetry: *Claiming Kin* (Wesleyan University Press, 1976), *The Forces of Plenty* (1983), *The Lotus Flowers* (1987), *Two Trees* (1992), *Kyrie* (1995), and *Shadow of Heaven* (2002), the last five of these from W. W. Norton. She is coeditor of an anthology of essays, *Poets Teaching Poets: Self and the World* (University of Michigan Press, 1996), and collected her own essays on craft in *The Flexible Lyric* (University of Georgia Press, 1999). She lives in Vermont and teaches in the low-residency MFA Program for Writers at Warren Wilson College. Her *New and Selected Poems* will appear in 2007.

DAVID WAGONER was born in Massillon, Ohio, in 1926, and grew up in Whiting, Indiana. He has published seventeen books of poems, most recently *Good Morning and Good Night* (University of Illinois Press, 2005), and ten novels, one of which (*The Escape Artist*) was made into a movie by Francis Ford Coppola in 1982. He taught at the University of Washington for fifty-one years and edited *Poetry Northwest* for thirty-six of them.

Of "The Driver," Wagoner writes: "I've read many detective/crime/suspense novels in which bank robberies almost invariably go wrong (though John Dillinger didn't seem to have much trouble in my hometown), so I decided to write a poem whose plot was more rewarding to almost everyone involved."

CHARLES HARPER WEBB was born in Philadelphia, Pennsylvania, in 1952, and grew up in Houston, Texas. *Hot Popsicles*, his book of prose poems, was published by the University of Wisconsin Press in 2005, and his fifth book of verse, *Amplified Dog*, by Red Hen Press in 2006. He has received a Guggenheim Fellowship. A former rock singer, guitarist, and psychotherapist, Webb edited *Stand Up Poetry: An Expanded Anthology* (University of Iowa Press, 2002). He directs the MFA program at California State University, Long Beach.

Of "Prayer to Tear the Sperm-Dam Down," Webb writes: "I read Suzanne Paola's 'Prayer to Seal Up the Wombdoor' soon after the birth of my son. Being a natural contrarian, I began my own Prayer in simple opposition: You want to seal the wombdoor? Fine! I want to open it up. But the poem quickly grew into a celebration of the selfish human drive to reproduce and live on our unconscious, hence indifferent, Earth. As a new parent, I felt a deepened connection with my own parents—who couldn't easily have sealed up Mom's womb door even if they'd wanted to—and of their parents, and theirs, and theirs . . . I found myself saying things that I, while childless by choice, never thought I'd ever say. If the sense of fun, excitement, and energy I felt giving birth to this poem comes through to the reader, it may become another argument for the worthiness-to-live of humankind."

C. K. WILLIAMS was born in Newark, New Jersey, in 1936. He is the author of nine books of poetry, the most recent of which, *The Singing*, won the National Book Award for 2003. His previous book, *Repair*, was awarded the 2000 Pulitzer Prize, and his collection *Flesh and Blood* received the National Book Critics Circle Award. These were published by Farrar, Straus and Giroux. His *Collected Poems* will appear in 2006. He has published translations of Sophocles' *Women of Trachis*, Euripides' *Bacchae*, and poems of Francis Ponge. His book of essays, *Poetry and Consciousness* (University of Michigan Press), appeared in 1998, and a memoir, *Misgivings* (Farrar, Straus and Giroux), in 2000. He teaches in the creative writing program at Princeton University.

Of "Ponies," Williams writes: "Some poems have many ulterior motives, others not. If this poem has any, they're more restrained than is the case with much of my work. The ponies were in a field not far from our house in France, I'd often pass them on my evening bike ride, and once in the late dusk I was struck by the silence in which they moved, the timelessness they seemed to exist within, and how close they were in their behavior to the ancient horses that would have roamed that part of the world through all the time of human existence. All of this arrived more as a mood, an atmosphere, than a series of perceptual thoughts, and the working out of the poem had to do with getting its elements separated, then put together again. It wasn't as easy as it might perhaps seem."

TERENCE WINCH was born in the Bronx in 1945. He has lived in and around Washington, D.C., for many years. He has made his living as a musician, writer, and editor. His last book is a collection of nonfiction stories called *That Special Place: New World Irish Stories* (Hanging Loose, 2004), centered on his experiences playing traditional Irish music. A new collection of poems, *Boy Drinkers*, will be out in 2007, also from Hanging Loose.

Of "Sex Elegy," Winch writes: "The poem is a lament over the passage of time. People disappear from our lives, intimacy turns into distance, yet because the past stays present in our memories, present and past coexist simultaneously in our minds. That paradox is at the heart of this poem. In 'Sex Elegy,' the past wins out."

SUSAN WOOD was born in 1946 in Commerce, Texas (a deeply American name in its hopefulness—there is little commerce there). She is the author of three collections of poems: *Asunder* (Penguin, 2001), *Campo Santo* (Louisiana State University Press, 1991), and *Bazaar* (Henry Holt, 1981). Her poems were selected for *The Pushcart Prize 2000* and *The Best American Poetry 2000*. She was a Guggenheim Fellow in 1998–99. She is the Gladys Louise Fox Professor of English at Rice University in Houston.

Wood writes: "I spent several months writing on Martha's Vineyard and the walk described in the poem is one I frequently took with my dog. 'Gratification' was one of those lucky poems that came to me quickly, almost fully formed. I'd been lonely there at first, but had grown enchanted with the place and the space to write, and the afternoon I wrote this poem was, for some reason, particularly magical. I felt blessed. And saved, somehow. Shortly after I started writing poems as a college student, my mother said to someone, 'Why can't she write any happy poems?' Well, Mother, if you're out there somewhere, I can. We all grow up."

FRANZ WRIGHT was born in Vienna, Austria, in 1953, but grew up in the Pacific Northwest, the Midwest, and California. He received the 2004 Pulitzer Prize for *Walking to Martha's Vineyard* (Knopf, 2003). Other books include *Ill Lit: New & Selected Poems* (Oberlin College Press, 1998) and his newest collection, *God's Silence* (Knopf, 2006). He is poet-in-residence at Brandeis University.

Of "A Happy Thought," Wright writes: "This poem was written one morning in Fayetteville, Arkansas, where I was living in the spring of 2004. It was written very quickly, in a half hour or so (unlike most of my poems, which generally take weeks, months, or years to finish)—perhaps because I noticed right away that the lines were presenting themselves in a more or less iambic manner and that the whole feel of the poem, spatially, in its particular rhymes or off-rhymes and the semirepetition of lines bore some distant resemblance to the villanelle. So once that was established, and I had a rough sense of how long the poem should be, I was able to proceed in an improvisatory way, and after producing several variants to recognize the one that was most successful in terms of both music and sense."

ROBERT WRIGLEY was born in 1951 in East St. Louis, Illinois, and grew up not far away, in Collinsville, a coal-mining town. Since 1974 he has lived in the West, mostly in northern Idaho, where he directs the graduate writing program at the University of Idaho. He is the author of seven books of poems, including most recently *Earthly Meditations: New and Selected Poems* (2006). His previous collections include *Lives of the Animals* (2003), *Reign of Snakes* (1999), and *In the Bank of Beautiful Sins* (1995), all from Penguin. He lives with his wife, the writer Kim Barnes, in the woods near Moscow, Idaho.

Of "Religion," Wrigley writes: "I remember hearing the late William Stafford say, with a wry tone in his voice and a half-smile on his face, 'The hardest thing in the world to write about is a dead dog,' and although it has taken me too many decades to learn my hard lesson, I am now able to avoid conversations about religion at dinner parties. Which is to say, I'm still extremely fond of dogs, especially those one might refer to as 'faithful.'"

DAVID YEZZI was born in Albany, New York, in 1966. His books of poetry are *Sad Is Eros* (Aralia Press, 2003) and *The Hidden Model* (TriQuarterly/Northwestern University Press, 2003). His libretto for a chamber opera by David Conte, *Firebird Motel*, was performed in 2003. A former director of the Unterberg Poetry Center of the 92nd Street Y in New York City, he is executive editor of *The New Criterion*.

Of "The Call," Yezzi writes: "As an acting student many years ago, I was given an exercise that ran roughly as follows: facing a partner, study his or her face, choosing something that you love about it, the curve of a lip, perhaps, or a wisp of hair. Continue to examine their face, next choosing something silly about its appearance, something that makes you laugh, a freckle or a crooked tooth. Finally, choose something that you hate: a patch of dry skin, some split ends. Now close your eyes and recall the various facial features: the beloved, the silly, the loathed. The hated feature often returned most easily and clearly, and it tended to produce, not repulsion, but tenderness. Something of this unexpected reversal underlies 'The Call.'"

DEAN YOUNG was born in Columbia, Pennsylvania, in 1955. He has published six books of poems, most recently *Elegy on Toy Piano* (Pittsburgh University Press, 2005). A new book, *embryoyo*, will be published in 2006 by Believer Books. He has received fellowships from the National Endowment for the Arts and the Guggenheim Foundation. He teaches in the Iowa Writers' Workshop and in the Warren Wilson low-residency MFA program.

Of "Clam Ode," Young writes: "One of the biggest challenges this poem presented was how not to confuse the spelling of clam and calm. In fact the poem grew out of my problems distinguishing the two words. I guess one of the reasons I write poems is to have the chance to make the best of all my disabilities, quirks, weirdnesses, indirect assays, hawks, and handsaws. That's what makes trying to write a poem that endeavors to build an argument, to work through an idea, absurdly appealing. My own inadequacy at doing such a thing gives me liberty."

Alaska Quarterly Review, poetry ed. Ronald Spatz. University of Alaska, 3211 Providence Drive, Anchorage, AK 99508.

American Poetry Review, eds. Stephen Berg, David Bonanno, and Arthur Vogelsang. 117 S. 17th St., Ste 910, Philadelphia, PA 19103.

Atlanta Review, ed. Dan Veach. PO Box 8248, Atlanta, GA 31106.

The Atlantic Monthly, poetry ed. David Barber. PO Box 130149, Boston, MA 02113.

Barrow Street, eds. Patricia Carlin, Peter Covino, Lois Hirshkowitz, and Melissa Hotchkiss. PO Box 1831, New York, NY 10156.

Boulevard, ed. Richard Burgin. 6614 Clayton Rd., Box 325, Richmond Heights, MO 63117.

The Briar Cliff Review, ed. Tricia Currans-Sheehan. 3303 Rebecca St., Sioux City, IA 51104-2100.

The Canary, eds. Joshua Edwards, Anthony Robinson, and Nick Twemlow. 573 E. 17th Ave., Eugene, OR 97401.

The Cincinnati Review, poetry ed. Don Bogen. PO Box 210069, Cincinnati, OH 45221-0069.

Columbia Poetry Review, English Dept., Columbia College, 600 S. Michigan Ave., Chicago, IL 60605.

The Connecticut Review, ed. John Briggs. English Dept., Western Connecticut State University, 181 White St., Danbury, CT 06810.

Crab Orchard Review, ed. Allison Joseph. Dept. of English, Faner Hall 2380, Mail Code 4503, Southern Illinois University, 1000 Faner Dr., Carbondale, IL 62901.

Crazyhorse, poetry eds. Carol Ann Davis and Garrett Doherty. Dept. of English, College of Charleston, 66 George St., Charleston, SC 29424.

CROWD, ed. Aimee Kelly; poetry ed. Brett Fletcher Lauer. PO Box 1373, New York, NY 10276.

Ecotone, poetry ed. Sally Smits. Creative Writing Dept., University of North Carolina at Wilmington, 601 S. College Rd., Wilmington, NC 28403-3297.

Endicott Review, ed. Dan Sklar. Endicott College, 376 Hale Street, Beverly, MA 01915.

Failbetter, poetry ed. Meghan Cleary. http://www.failbetter.com

Field, eds. Pamela Alexander, Martha Collins, David Walker, and David Young. Oberlin College Press, 50 N. Professor St., Oberlin, OH 44074-1091.

Five Points, poetry eds. David Bottoms, Megan Sexton, Beth Gylys. Georgia State University, PO Box 3999, Atlanta, GA 30302-3999.

Fulcrum, eds. Philip Nikolayev and Katia Kapovich. 334 Harvard St., Ste D-2, Cambridge, MA 02139.

Georgia Review, ed. T. R. Hummer. University of Georgia, Athens, GA 30602-9009.

Gettysburg Review, ed. Peter Stitt. Gettysburg College, Gettysburg, PA 17325-1491.

Gulf Coast, poetry eds. Darin Ciccotelli, Emily Pérez, and Bradford Telford. English Dept., University of Houston, Houston, TX 77204-3013.

Harvard Review, poetry ed. Don Share. Lamont Library, Harvard University, Cambridge, MA 02138.

The Hat, eds. Jordan Davis and Chris Edgar. 1793 Riverside Dr. #3B, New York, NY 10034.

Hayden's Ferry Review, poetry eds. Laura Cruser and Brian Leary. Virginia G. Piper Center for Creative Writing, Box 875002, Arizona State University, Tempe, AZ 85287-5002.

Iodine Poetry Journal, ed. Jonathan K. Rice. PO Box 18548, Charlotte, NC 28218-0548.

The Iowa Review, ed. David Hamilton. 308 EPB, University of Iowa, Iowa City, IA 52242.

The Kenyon Review, poetry ed. David Baker. http://www.kenyonreview.org

LIT, ed. Justin Marks, poetry ed. Joseph Housley. New School Writing Program, 66 W. 12th St., Rm 508, New York, NY 10011.

Margie, ed.-in-chief Robert Nazarene, senior ed. James Wilson. PO Box 250, Chesterfield, MO 63006-0250.

Michigan Quarterly Review, ed. Laurence Goldstein. 3574 Rackham Bldg., 915 E. Washington St., Ann Arbor, MI 48109-1070.

MiPoesias, poetry ed. Amy King. http://www.mipoesias.com

New American Writing, eds. Maxine Chernoff and Paul Hoover. 369 Molino Ave., Mill Valley, CA 94941.

The New Criterion, ed. David Yezzi. 900 Broadway, Ste 602, New York, NY 10003.

New England Review, poetry ed. C. Dale Young. Middlebury College, Middlebury, VT 05753.

New Letters, ed. Robert Stewart. UMKC University House, 5101 Rockhill Rd., Kansas City, MO 64110-2499.

The New Yorker, poetry ed. Alice Quinn. 4 Times Square, New York, NY 10036.

Nightsun, managing ed. Gerry La Femina, guest ed. Stephen Dunn. Frostburg Center for Creative Writing, Dept. of English, Frostburg State University, Frostburg, MD 21532.

The Paris Review, poetry eds. Meghan O'Rourke and Charles Simic. 62 White St., New York, NY 10013.

Poetry, ed. Christian Wiman. 1030 N. Clark St., Ste 420, Chicago, IL 60610.

Poetry Daily, eds. Rob Anderson, Diane Boller, and Don Selby. http://www.poems.com.

POOL: A Journal of Poetry, eds. Patty Seyburn and Judith Taylor. PO Box 49738, Los Angeles, CA 90049.

Rhino, eds. Helen Degen Cohen, Alice George, Kathleen Kirk, and Deborah Nodler Rosen. The Poetry Forum, Inc., PO Box 591, Evanston, IL 60204.

River Styx, ed. Richard Newman. 3547 Olive St., Ste 107, St. Louis, MO 63103-1014.

Shenandoah, ed. R. T. Smith. Mattingly House, 2 Lee Ave., Washington and Lee University, Lexington, VA 24450-0303.

Shiny, ed. Michael Friedman. PO Box 13125, Denver, CO 80201.

Subtropics, poetry ed. Sidney Wade. PO Box 112075, 4008 Turlington Hall, University of Florida, Gainesville, FL 32611-2075.

Third Coast, poetry eds. Jason Olsen and Roy Seeger. Dept. of English, Western Michigan University, Kalamazoo, MI 49008-5331.

Verse, eds. Brian Henry and Andrew Zawacki. English Dept., University of Richmond, Richmond, VA 23173.

Virginia Quarterly Review, ed. Ted Genoways, poetry chair David Lee Rubin. University of Virginia, One West Range, Box 400223, Charlottesville, VA 22904-4223.

ACKNOWLEDGMENTS

The series editor wishes to thank Mark Bibbins for his invaluable assistance. Shanna Compton, James Cummins, Steven Dube, Deborah Landau, and Michael Schiavo made useful suggestions or helped in other ways. Warm thanks go also to Glen Hartley, Lynn Chu, and Farah Peterson of Writers' Representatives, and to Alexis Gargagliano, Molly Dorozenski, Erich Hobbing, and John McGhee of Scribner.

Grateful acknowledgment is made of the magazines in which these poems first appeared and the magazine editors who selected them. A sincere attempt has been made to locate all copyright holders. Unless otherwise noted, copyright to the poems is held by the individual poets.

Kim Addonizio: "Verities" appeared in *Poetry*. Reprinted by permission of the poet.

Dick Allen: "'See the Pyramids Along the Nile'" appeared in *Boulevard*. Reprinted by permission of the poet.

Craig Arnold: Part 11 of "Couple from Hell" appeared in *Barrow Street*. Reprinted by permission of the poet.

John Ashbery: "A Worldly Country" appeared in *The New Yorker*. Reprinted by permission of the poet.

Jesse Ball: "Speech in a Chamber" appeared in *The Paris Review*. Reprinted by permission of the poet.

Krista Benjamin, "Letter from My Ancestors" appeared in *Margie*. Reprinted by permission of the poet.

Ilya Bernstein: "You Must Have Been a Beautiful Baby" appeared in *Fulcrum*. Reprinted by permission of the poet.

Gaylord Brewer: "Apologia to the Blue Tit" appeared in *The Briar Cliff Review* and in *River Styx*. Reprinted by permission of the poet.

Tom Christopher: "Rhetorical Figures" appeared in *Hayden's Ferry Review*. Reprinted by permission of the poet.

Laura Cronk: "Sestina for the Newly Married" appeared in *LIT*. Reprinted by permission of the poet.

Carl Dennis: "Our Generation" appeared in *The Kenyon Review*. Reprinted by permission of the poet.

Stephen Dobyns: "Toward Some Bright Moment" from *Mystery, So*

Katia Kapovich: "The Ferry" appeared in *Harvard Review*. Reprinted by permission of the poet.

Laura Kasischke: "At Gettysburg" appeared in *New England Review*. Reprinted by permission of the poet.

Joy Katz: "Just a second ago" appeared in *The Cincinnati Review*. Reprinted by permission of the poet.

David Kirby: "Seventeen Ways from Tuesday" appeared in *Subtropics*. Reprinted by permission of the poet.

Jennifer L. Knox: "The Laws of Probability in Levittown" appeared in *The Hat*. Reprinted by permission of the poet.

Ron Koertge: "Found" appeared in *Iodine Poetry Journal*. Reprinted by permission of the poet.

John Koethe: "Sally's Hair" from *Sally's Hair*. © 2006 by John Koethe. Reprinted by permission of HarperCollins. First appeared in *The Kenyon Review*.

Mark Kraushaar: "Tonight" appeared in *The Gettysburg Review*. Reprinted by permission of the poet.

Julie Larios: "Double Abecedarian: Please Give Me" appeared in *The Georgia Review*. Reprinted by permission of the poet.

Dorianne Laux: "Demographic" appeared in *Alaska Quarterly Review*. Reprinted by permission of the poet.

Reb Livingston: "That's Not Butter" appeared in *MiPoesias*. Reprinted by permission of the poet.

Thomas Lux: "Eyes Scooped Out and Replaced by Hot Coals" appeared in *Five Points*. Reprinted by permission of the poet.

Paul Muldoon: "Blenheim" appeared in *Five Points*. Reprinted by permission of the poet.

Marilyn Nelson: "Albert Hinckley" appeared in *The Cincinnati Review*. Reprinted by permission of the poet.

Richard Newman: "Briefcase of Sorrow" from *Borrowed Towns*. © 2005 by Richard Newman. Reprinted by permission of Word Press. First appeared in *Crab Orchard Review*.

Mary Oliver: "The Poet with His Face in His Hands" from *New and Selected Poems, Volume Two*. © 2005 by Mary Oliver. Reprinted by permission of Beacon Press, Boston. First appeared in *The New Yorker*.

Danielle Pafunda: "Small Town Rocker" appeared in *The Canary*. Reprinted by permission of the poet.

Mark Pawlak: "The Sharper the Berry" from *Official Versions*. © 2006 by Mark Pawlak. Reprinted by permission of Hanging Loose Press. First appeared in *New American Writing*.

Bao Phi: "Race" appeared in *Michigan Quarterly Review*. Reprinted by permission of the poet.

Donald Platt: "Two Poets Meet" appeared in *The Iowa Review*. Reprinted by permission of the poet.

Lawrence Raab: "The Great Poem" appeared in *Nightsun*. Reprinted by permission of the poet.

Betsy Retallack: "Roadside Special" appeared in *Endicott Review*. Reprinted by permission of the poet.

Liz Rosenberg: "The Other Woman's Point of View" appeared in *The Kenyon Review*. Reprinted by permission of the poet.

J. Allyn Rosser: "Discounting Lynn" appeared in *Failbetter*. Reprinted by permission of the poet.

Kay Ryan: "Thin" from *The Niagara River*. © 2005 by Kay Ryan. Reprinted by permission of Grove Press. First appeared in *Poetry*.

Mary Jo Salter: "A Phone Call to the Future" appeared in *The Georgia Review*. Reprinted by permission of the poet.

Vijay Seshadri: "Memoir" appeared in *The New Yorker*. Reprinted by permission of the poet.

Alan Shapiro: "Misjudged Fly Ball" appeared in *The Cincinnati Review*. Reprinted by permission of the poet.

Charles Simic: "House of Cards" appeared in *Virginia Quarterly Review*. Reprinted by permission of the poet.

Gerald Stern: "Homesick" appeared in *Ecotone*. Reprinted by permission of the poet.

James Tate: "The Loser" appeared in *Crazyhorse*. Reprinted by permission of the poet.

Sue Ellen Thompson: "Body English" appeared in *The Connecticut Review*. Reprinted by permission of the poet.

Tony Towle: "Misprision" appeared in *LIT*. Reprinted by permission of the poet.

Alison Townsend: "What I Never Told You About the Abortion" appeared in *Margie*. Reprinted by permission of the poet.

Paul Violi: "Counterman" appeared in *Shiny*. Reprinted by permission of the poet.

Ellen Bryant Voigt: "Harvesting the Cows" appeared in *The Kenyon Review*. Reprinted by permission of the poet.

David Wagoner: "The Driver" appeared in *Margie*. Reprinted by permission of the poet.

Charles Harper Webb: "Prayer to Tear the Sperm-Dam Down"